Poems from
The Lockdown

ii

EDITOR'S NOTE

On 13th April I first attempted to publish, through Amazon KDP, an anthology entitled "Covid-19: Poems from The Lockdown". Amazon KDP rejected this on the basis that it included references to Covid-19, and it broke their publication guidelines meaning they were unable to offer the book for sale.

On 18th April, a new version, which removed the words COVID-19 from the title and all administrative references within the book was put forward. This was called "Poems from the Lockdown – January to April 2020". This too was rejected.

Below are both rejection emails.

Alert from Amazon KDP Content Review 13/04/2020,
Hello,

We're contacting you regarding the following book(s): Covid-19: Poems from The Lockdown by Mariangela Canzi (AUTHOR); Trevor Maynard (AUTHOR) (ID: PRI-AF0E4ZSHAN6)

Your book does not comply with our guidelines. As a result we are not offering your book for sale.

Due to the rapidly changing nature of information around the COVID-19 virus, we are referring customers to official sources for health information about the virus.

Please consider removing references to COVID-19 for this book. Amazon reserves the right to determine what content we offer according to our content guidelines.

You can find our content guidelines on the KDP website:
https://lnkd.in/gk4wCuk

Amazon KDP

Alert from Amazon KDP Content Review 18/04/2020,
00.21
Hello,

We're contacting you regarding the following book(s):

Poems from The Lockdown: January to April 2020 by Mariangela Canzi
(AUTHOR); Cigeng Zhang (AUTHOR); Cary Barney (AUTHOR); Geraldine
Moorkens Byrne (AUTHOR); Neetu Malik (AUTHOR); Robert Eugene Rubino
(AUTHOR); Syble Heffernan (AUTHOR); Susana H Case (AUTHOR); and
over one hundred others (AUTHOR); Trevor Maynard (AUTHOR) (ID: PRI-
AF0E4ZSHAN6)

Your book does not comply with our guidelines. As a result we are not offering
your book for sale.

 Due to the rapidly changing nature of information around the COVID-19 virus,
we are referring customers to official sources for health information about the
virus. Please consider removing references to COVID-19 for this book.

Amazon reserves the right to determine what content we offer according to
our content guidelines. You can find our content guidelines on the KDP
website: https://kdp.amazon.com/help/topic/G200672390

Amazon KDP

A third attempt is being made whereby all references to
Covid-19, from the promotional description on the
Amazon.com website, has been removed. **This means the
only references to Covid-19 in the anthology are within
certain poems.**

If you, the anthology reader, are now reading this, which is
the third attempt at publication, and I hope you are, it
means that Amazon have finally accepted that poets are
allowed to talk about Covid-19, and the general public have
been allowed to read poetry on the subject of Covid-19. It
means that Amazon have honoured the constitutional right
to freedom of speech. I truly hope, you are reading this, so
that you may explore, enjoy and share the 146 poems from
115 poets which are included in this anthology.

Editors' Update – 20th April 2020

Amazon approved the revised copy of "Poems from the Lockdown", accepting the work of 115 poets, writing from the heart, at this incredibly difficult time for our world.

At Willowdown Books (UK), we truly believe it is very important that these voices are heard, and that poetry is indeed the soul of humanity. We believe this anthology, and other poetry, as well as fiction, oral history, documentary, and reportage, will contribute to the historical document of these unprecedented times that will give not only an honest and true perspective, but also a greater understanding of our experience of the global pandemic of 2020.

Stay Safe, love, light and peace, always.

vi

For our daughter Doctor Samantha Steele, all the other medical staff and key workers, as well as those who have been kind and supportive of their fellow human beings in this global time of crisis.

In Memory of Sara Cupp Smith 20th Nov 1946 to 14th April 2020) who was married to Richard Glen Smith for 52 years. Sara contributed two poems to this anthology, and Richard, one.

Sara and Glen "your poetry is honest and true" thank you for sharing.

Copyright Notice

Poems from The Lockdown

© Willowdown Books 2020

Willowdown Books asserts its copyright of this book as an anthology, by which is meant this collection of poems. Willowdown Books asserts no copyright over any of the individual poems.

Each author has agreed to give Willlowdown Books permission to publish their poem(s) only within the anthology, in any media, and to use their name and poem(s) in any marketing or promotional activity which pertains to the marketing and promotion of the anthology. Willowdown Books cannot print or use any other media to publish any poem from the anthology individually, except with the express permission of the author.

The copyright of the individual poem is that of the author solely. For use of an individual poem, in any media, please contact the individual author.

Copyright is asserted (by both Willowdown Books and the individual authors) under the Copyright Laws of the British Commonwealth of Nations, the United States of America and all the countries of the Berne and Universal Copyright Conventions. All rights, including Stage, Motion Picture, Television, Public Reading, Translation into foreign language, any Internet or related media is strictly reserved (by the author, or Willowdown Books as detailed above).

Poems from The Lockdown
Maynard, Trevor (Ed.)
Willowdown Books
ISBN-13 9798638251031

Acknowledgements

Thank you to all those who have shared their poems. For my wife, Jo, not only for her tireless contribution to the work, but also her encouragement, enthusiasm, and love. Thank you to my family, and friends; for their love, and support, and a special thank you to Mariangela Canzi Camille Hill, Maxine Nodel, Michael Hatchett, Cary Barney, Kayla Matheson, Susan Fleming, and Diane Burrow for their additional contributions. Keep Safe.

Foreword

Poems from the Lockdown (2020)

I was inspired to put together this anthology of poems by my communications with the LinkedIn Group *Poetry, Review, and Discuss*; in particular, the following contribution posted by Mariangela Canzi, which is dedicated to her friend, Dr. Norman Jones, who died on 27th March.

Silence

Isolated from the world,
I look in wonder...
Lonely streets
tender grass
chatty birds...
Silence.
A tricky enemy
is crushing us
deep within.
Covid-19
is killing people
wildly.
Silence.
Death is coming on.
In the weeping sky
gloom and woe
are flying up.
Trees are whispering
a song of grief.

Mariangela is a regular contributor to the group, and has had several poems published in The Poetic Bond series. She has been locked down in Italy since March 9th, with Spain, France, Spain and much of the rest of Europe following.

In the UK, 'Lockdown' started on March 23rd, 2020, although there is a less clear picture in the *federal* USA, Many people there have taken it upon themselves to act, self-isolate, and to remain safe and well.

Social media has proved, for most part, a boon in this difficult time; with the additional bonus that some people are *actually* talking more to their family (if only through screens) than they might ordinarily.

'Lockdown' has also given people the opportunity to create; one of the prime reasons for this book is to give an outlet for that creativity, to allow the sharing of experiences through that most empathic of the arts, poetry. The paperback will be available through Amazon, and I am working on a multi-part Kindle version. Poetry is notoriously difficult to format to Kindle, specifically some of the diverse forms which can be seen, and are encouraged, in this volume.

Thank you to everyone who has shared their work; stay well, stay safe, and keep writing and reading.

Trevor Maynard 11 April 2020.

xiv

Poems from The Lockdown

Contents

1. Social Distance

When the Music Begins	12
In My Solitude	13
The New Normal	14
Quarantine Routine	15
Old words, new tricks	16
Social Distancing *(speak to me)*	17
Social Distancing *(every two minutes)*	18
Social Distancing *(eyes like prey)*	19
Wide Berth	20
Thoughts at the Time of the Virus - Pandemic	21
The Walk	23
Waiting Alone	24
Not Airborne	25
Shutdown	27
Grocery Shopping Whole Foods	28
Lockdown Pheromone	29
Routine	31
"After the Pandemic"	32

2. Inside

Let's all dance in the street	36
Applause *(Madrid, March 2020)*	37
Field Notes from More Than Likely COVID19	38
Life in the Time of Coronavirus	39
Prison Life	40
Podcast	41
The Hunkering Down	43
Click	45
When Screens Replace Touch	46
Inside and Outside	47
Inside Out	48
Looking Outside	49
Make an Effort, Make Your Bed	50
#selfcareinthetimeofcorona	51
Backpacks	52
Day 16 of Quarantine: Breathe	53
Eleven Days:	
Living Under a 21st Century Pandemic	55
Once More	57
Stuck in the Funhouse	58

3. Virus

Adrenalin Rush	62
Seduction by Virus	63
Exposed	64
In Today's News	65
Cosmic Awareness	67
The Thing with No Form	68
Corona Pantoum	69
Bubbles in a War Zone	70
What if	71
To A Plague Rat	72
Intubed	73
During My Illness	75
Intubation	76
A Pandemic Day	77
Then the World Changed	78
Pandemic *(we are many)*	79
Pandemic *(I hear my father's voice)*	80
Rights	83
Black Swan Song	85
What is left	86

4. Wry

Shop-fever	90
Pretend You're a Dangerous Dissident	91
Leaves Me Breathless	92
troubadours of the scaffold	93
Which Way is Up?	94
The Lilac Bush	95
Cyanthropic Daze	96
The end of the world from inside the house	97
Covid-19 Lockdown	98
the dishes	99
Shouldn't We Have Enough	100
What if My Surreal is Your Surreal	101
Hardly an Apocalypse in Here	102
Battered Ego	103
Prepped	105
Not a Number	107
breathe	108
The Three Stages of Social Distancing	109
Five Directions for Surviving COVID-19	110

5. Art

Postcards We Never Sent	114
Bouleversée/turned upside down	115
Space Bubbles	116
Blossoms	117
#quarantineartclub	118
Actually	123
Lockdown	125
In and Out of Quarantine with Persephone	127
Isolation Poem with the Destruction of Pompeii	129
Ophiostoma ulmi	130
The Song is Quiet Now	131
Day 18 of Quarantine: Perspectives	133
100,000	135
unwitting conquests	136

6. Those Close

Moments of Life	140
Isolation	141
grasp-less	142
Seeds in the Desert	143
Inundated	145
Isolation Poem with Ceres	147
Once Upon a Childrens' Game	148
Essential	149
Paranoid Hopeless Romantic *(March 10th 2020)*	150
Reflecting on another time of separation	151
To My Son	152
When Will He Grow Wings	153
Now That You're Gone	154
In Sickness and In Health	155
Redemption	157
No Time for Spoon River *(To the Victims of COVID-19)*	159

7. Socio Politico

Sheltering	164
Crossing the Delaware	165
A Cadence Inverted	167
Tsunami	169
Just a Nurse	172
Looking for Normal	173
N-95	175
Dog Walking in the Global Pandemic	177
Making Anagrams Great Again	179
"This is a War"	181
Go	183
We didn't think it would be us next	184
United States of Virus	185
What if my surreal is your surreal?	186

8. This Spring

The World has Changed, But There is Hope	190
In These Times We Keep	191
Speak to me of new	192
Never-ending Sun	193
Pandemic (5) - Possibilities	194
Hope	195
Spring 2020	196
A Prayer for the Sequestered	197
the morrow	198
After	199
This Spring	201
And's and But's of Quarantine	203
3/11/20	205
Spring Postponed *(a Haiku sequence)*	206

9. Nature

Those Eyes of Mine	210
Shelter in Place	211
The Frozen Spring	212
Settlement	213
A Fallout unspoken	214
'tween times	215
Vernal Equinox Lockdown	216
Anthropocene Sin	217
Tiny Bay	219
An Echo Through Pelagic	221
All Back in Place	223
Maybe we will all become butterflies	224

Appendix

Alphabetical index of first lines	228
Alphabetical list of poets' biographies	236
The Poetic Bond Series	266
The Cunningham Short Story Competition	270
Willowdown Books Catalogue	272

9

1
Social
Distance

11

When the Music Begins

The day is chilly and grey and eerie,
as if the sky inched away from its blue,
and our collective grief evaporated and
turned into the clouds hovering heavily

above our heads, loaded with the sensation
of imminent tears—lump-throated and ready
to burst. The silence is infused with the scent
of our held in breath, full of waiting, and the

trees are beginning to bloom, not knowing if
it's alright to unleash the full force of their color
into bleak eyes looped with nightfall. A man
walking across the street didn't smile at me

like he usually does, as if even that tiny, brief
sun couldn't rise this morning, and his dog's
tail wasn't wagging, like it had been scolded for
continuing to dance. Tomorrow, I hope to hear

children playing joyfully in the distance—
that it's ok to feel your heart beating, as many
are coming to a heart-wrenching stop. That
it's ok to laugh uncontrollably and fill the

loneliness of a room with something outside
of the body. Tomorrow, I hope we feel less
fear, because it cripples the hands we use
to catch each other. Courage is contagious

too. The dark only knows how to scribble,
but we know how to paint from the palette
of our pain. Tomorrow, I hope we hug those
we love in ways more tender than touch,

and songs slip out from between our clattering
teeth, and just like wind chimes, when there's
                              shivering, the music   begins

Andreas Fleps

In My Solitude

In the intersection of three circles, I live on free samples. You're not in the intersection of these circles are you? I will have at most one fistfight in at most one parking lot, as sure as Post Hoc is my name. Just change the channel, I say, as the seven billionth wonder of the world goes stomping off. It's 3 a.m. on Guam. Do you know where on Guam your intimations of love are? Of seven standers-by statistically one stands on one's own hands.

As walking in the acid rain, I'm packing ellipsoids more densely than I'm packing habitats, I'm not the kind of flightless bird that turns lights on and off for no good reason and the square of my agglomeration is commensurate with the cube root of my pursuit of sadness. There are more criteria for kickability than I can shake a stick at. Caught with my hand in the funerary urn I lose my chance to factor in that final ash.

As weighing options is a prelude to abstention, I, a lamp, might go out empty handed. Yet to be a hero and unsung, the probability that I assign to no straight line is one. I throw endangered species to the wind. I think outside the singularity. I will not be falsely accused. I saw him just last century and he seemed fine. Where we are going what need will we have of bodies that are not convex? It's nuance versus subtlety, no grudge match. May the maid of honor cut the cake and may the maid of honor never loose.

Heikki Houtari

The New Normal

broadway is dark
stores are closed
social distancing
is imposed

stay locked inside
shelter in place
six feet away
don't touch your face

disinfect your hands
wash your clothes
is that a sniffle?
elbow your nose

binge on Netflix
all day long
hold back tears
try to stay strong

watch the news
who's to blame?
pointing fingers
calling names

missing the hugs
of family and friends
wondering how
this all may end

life has changed
it's only temporary
we must have faith
though very scary

our new normal
since covid 19
a viral pandemic
the world's never seen.

Abby DeSantis

Quarantine Routine

We have broken down our morning to the essentials:
ignoring the dog
four layers of blankets
and sex.

At some point you'll pull me from the bed
I'll beat instant coffee grounds in water
in a way that makes me feel too much like my mother
I let you take the eggs—you were always better at them anyway

You make note of the provisions
a fridge overflowing
with the absence of buttermilk, 2%,
whipping cream

It's not your fault I've lost the ability to meditate;
blame it on intrusive thoughts, our collective exhale drowned out
by the rush of cars flooding down Richmond like a bloodstream.
For the first time we'll acknowledge my broken pancreas
as kind of a problem—but only because it makes you worry a bit
too much

We're doing what we can:
making sure we eat three times a day
stay hydrated
exercise (though that's mostly just you)

I promise we won't leave the place unless it's needed—
the trash lays dormant for nineteen days

and you still awake, timing my breathing.
Don't worry sweetheart, I'm not going anywhere;
we've got yesterday's cold brew to drink.

Danielle Solo

Old Words, New Tricks

Before
Social distancing might have meant
taking a quick break from Instagram
Corona was a beer you'd order with friends at a Mexican restaurant
Chugging as you chatted and crunched chips dripping with hot salsa
Flatten the curve was what I aimed for while sweating in spin class
Legs pumping up and down with twenty others
Inhaling and exhaling the same soggy air
Self-isolate would have been staying in one Friday night
Getting lost in a movie before bursting back outside the next morning
Lockdowns were drills that happened at schools
Or buildings in case there were intruders
We'd huddle together in the designated safe room,
Waiting and whispering until it ended
Quarantine was a horror movie that we watched one Halloween
Cuddling under a blanket, popping M&Ms
And holding in screams at the scary parts
Pandemic was a term you'd learn in history class,
Something from 1900s Europe
Where men in black and white photos were laid out
In rows and rows of beds
None of this meant anything to our old lives
We wouldn't have believed the new ways
Our old words would be used

Felicia Zuniga

Social Distancing *(speak to me)*

speak to me—
tell me the textured story I long to hear, to see
what isn't there but don't
open your mouth; your words are potent drops of venom
dangling in this biting air and we've been told
by the powers that be to stay

six feet away—

we can't touch anymore—
but should I be shunned to say I ache for the tight clasp of your fingers
in mine, unspoken words that held and would never
let go (but did) and would I be wrong
to whisper that I want so much the bouldered foundation of your smile;

a bordered wall around just you and me?

now I can only imagine what's behind your mask,
what's hidden inside
this electric screen of distorted images I receive, yet I can still remember
the breath of our laughter once—
mixed together as multiformed icicles in skating rink air
when we
turned and twirled, arms outstretched and the world
only a blur but tell me—

when this is all over, will we find each other again?

Natasha N. Deonarian

Social Distancing (every two minutes)

we were already distant
before regulations came
and we were told to contain
ourselves in our space
to keep us protected
as if alienation were strange

eyes on handheld devices
sipping beer in breweries
dinner night with friends
usually blinking in the dark
on blue-lit screens

what's new about it?

it is easy, methinks, to keep
our eyes where our mind is
seldom where it should be
like my last lover who couldn't resist

checking on his phone
every two minutes
when he was with me

Neetu Malik

Social Distancing (eyes like prey)

It's one am before I decide
no one else will be awake
I emerge to dump garbage
the chute pulling down the bags
clearing its greedy throat
and then I see her:

sleek black hair
pink nightgown
and moving bags
she presses to her chest

a wooden door slams shut behind her.

We stay the recommended distance apart:
six feet for how far the infected droplets spread

and back up

slowly

pretend we have seen nothing

seen no one on this first official night
of government-recommended quarantine

until our hands rest again on doorknobs
and we jolt our heads back

eyes wide like prey
those of an accusatory animal

Danielle Solo

Wide Berth

Veiled beneath layers of mesh
Filtering out the tiniest of particles
Could be upturned lips, maybe?
That would mouth reassurance.

In their absence I seek the rest
of Duchenne's composition:
Vaulted cheeks meeting crow's feet.

But her eyes are cast down, hurrying past
A body's distance apart

Tanya Fraser

Thoughts at the Time of the Virus - Pandemic

"Each of us has the plague within him;
no one, no one on earth is free from it."
Albert Camus

I
We search for release in unimportant ways –
reach for fame, choose crude footpaths,
come away with nothing, hoard the fortune,
hide the prize,
no remedy, no relief, only solitary confinement.
It's not about flash, it's not about tinsel.
The old man's testament
parcels out his treasure – too late.

It's not about glitter, it's not about gold.

II

It's not about gold – it's a condition, not a decision.
When fevered bodies fail,
and ashen spirits sicken, show compassion.
The world, a *camera obscura*,
a darkened box where slender bands of light
enter a narrowed aperture –
where the larger sphere is viewed inverted,
reversed in blurred projection,
in masked and gloved disintegration,
nights dense with anxiety, agitation.
Outside air not felt inside the camera's eye.

The streets…are empty.

III

Streets and roads are empty –
no landmarks, no highway signs.
Draw feeble life from ashes – a shriveled spirit
lives in the night-time of the mind.
Imprisoned in this hidden world, dense
with unheard voices, I close my eyes in open space,
pay the toll, travel through…alone.

Patricia Williams

The Walk

We went walking
Socially distanced of course
Suddenly a 5-year-old biking
Stumbled and went off course

Down she went bike and all
Seemed like a pretty nasty fall
Her loud cries filled my heart
Instinctively I raced, letting down my guard

Any other time than this
I'd have picked her up in a beat
But this extraordinary spring
I stopped short- helpless -at six feet

I am a mother of two
It was against my core
But caution commanded
Doing less is more

My eyes scanned impatiently
For her dad far behind
As I weighed action and inaction
In my restless mind

I could have corona
And just not show it
She could have grandparents
I just don't know it

No cuts, she's moving
No immediate signs of alarm
So I stood by my oath
First do no harm!"

Parul Bhargava

Waiting Alone

If I washed my hands
for 20 seconds with soap
and hot water, scrubbing
vigorously, could I save

you? My world has frozen
like an old movie projector
stopped in between frames,
one frame imposed on the next,

not clear, the way my future
is not clear, not written, depends
on what I do next, how well I wash
and if I isolate my body,

tamp down longings to hold
you, see you smile when I run
my fingers through your hair,
smell the faint trace of Irish Spring

on your skin and be so close
I can watch your whiskers sprout.
It is spring, weeds and flowers push up
from where they lay hidden

over the dark winter. The birds
are raising a ruckus, making it hard
for me to sleep. Part of me resents
their chorus, while I am alone.

Isolated and living within quiet,
thoughts of saving the world
tumble into those of tossing
my granddaughter high, catching

her in my arms amid giggles,
and wriggles and the words,
"more gamma, do it again."

Loretta Tobin

Not Airborne

Covid-19

Not airborne, but outside still feels poisoned
As I step into the sunlight for some vitamin D.
Others, walking their dog, or just walking,
Are like zombies shambling around,
Aimless. Best avoided.

Nowhere to go. Just need to GET OUT.

The ones talking too close to each other—
— less than six feet away (I don't really know
what six feet looks like, but I understand it to mean
"as far as reasonably possible") —
they are the ones who would hide a zombie bite.

The parks are closed.
The first fine was administered to a woman in Point Pleasant.
She was found standing on the shore,
the whole park to herself. The most special
and **Very Important Woman** in the world, apparently.

She must have thought so.

I'd like to think that our dog at least is happy.
Early on we joked that he made the virus
so we'd all stay at home.
He didn't know the plague would end his puppy playdates.
We meet other dogs outside,
and we can let them sniff each other,
Pulling desperately at their leads,
Stretching their necks out to get a whiff of friendship.
So long as we and the owner of the other dog stay
A full two meters apart.

We return home, relieved, somehow.
At home, after washing our hands,
We can be free from paranoia
And take comfort in breathing in
The stale air of an uncontaminated home.

Roisin Boyle

Shutdown

Slowing down we stroll don't run
let's google each other side by side by side
you in your little house me in my apartment
me in my container you in your shelter
corona-silent street lamps switch off one by one
we have coffee, cat on feet
nobody escapes from here
nor to our closed borders duck-tape
covers every crack sanitize fingers and everything they touch
it is so peaceful
in a shut down country turn off the underfloor heating before I go
jump the very last train out of the city
is it peace when no child's laughter reverberates when cafés quietly
keep the machines off when no bombs disturb
when the pandemic menaces us away from festivals
a box of peace with nothing inside
a box of peace to dash your nose in
until thoughts go white
why own more than one single knife
is peacefully soundless
and a camp with 1500 tents
for 12.000 adults and 8000 kids
is never peaceful enough to complete the thought
of war between people
and virus

Cindy Lynn Brown

Grocery Shopping Whole Foods in the Time of Corona

The far-off war is here now. The Italians
are singing from their balconies. The neighbor
hoods are lit up with signs: heroes live here,
for all the necessary workers. Last night
on the news Shreveport rivaled
New Orleans for the most affected,
South Korea bouncing back best. We are
all being chewed on in something's
big cavern of a mouth. For this occasion
we dress up in gas masks and take our
own bags to the store. We look and grab.
No more finger fucking the packages,
no more light reading of the ingredients,
no more picking up same nearby, cheaper
and with a more intriguing font. We are
being submerged maybe in a spill of water.
We've been set down by God to fend for our
selves. Bending over the avocadoes,
I feel the homeless's contagion set over me,
a poverty not so much as things, but as essence.
Beside the kumquats and guava, we mince pass
each other as though each of us were ticking time bombs.
And even as pre plague, behind our masks, we are loathe to speak.

Dorie LaRue

Lockdown Pheromone

Mundanity curves over the cloud,
I am limited to the view
Of little children
Across my balcony-
Watching eternity
On television;
An ant colony
Chaining walnut crumbs
From my kitchen floor,
In a flat curve,
Not understanding
Social distancing,
They float around my feet
Cramps
Are unusual
There are no distances
To travel,
My shoes are mocking
My locked door
is Waiting
Till the stars

Glitter in my eyes,
Watching eternity
sink in the night
Connecting
In the calm pheromones
Of distances
Of air
My feet are an imagination
Floating stories
Of wide-open doors
Walking on wet grass
Unhinged
Shadowing clouds
In a Long distance
Relationships
Mock ordinary
Loneliness.

Nida
Sahar

Routine

Routine! Without it we'd be lost, as well we might
just thinking of preoccupation- filling slots.

I could pick up a trail from where I left it hanging
In the never-never sideboard of a mind of 'mights'.

There swings half a dress and quarter of a skirt,
A shirt with holes and zipper-less, a jacket collar,

bits and pieces, jigsaws of the past, on hangers of the lost.
stored away in case one day… and here it is at last!

Lockdown! Giving us a chance to air them all
Or throw them out as good ideas, once,

now out of date and done. So, try and find plots in walls,
the crack of a ceiling or the squeaking of a door,

or look beneath the cupboard floor, the current store
of ironed out ideas, for now there is a chance to muse.

Choose from piles of promise, all the while, do not neglect
the every-days that mark a time of waiting to forget again.

Diane Burrow

"After the Pandemic"

After the pandemic
when the virus is defeated
and it is safe to travel
I will go back to Sacramento.
To see my sister and her husband and children.
To see my friends going back to elementary school.
To see old familiar places.
To do silly things we used to do when I was a kid.
The places will still be there.
The houses, the streets.
The storefronts, the parks.
But I wonder how many of the people will be.
And of those that are,
how many will have been touched by tragedy?
When I think about that, the tears rise up behind my eyes
and I put my head in my hands and cry.

Camille Hill

33

2
Inside

35

Let's All Dance in the Streets

I am the elder.
They ask me to stay in the house
And no one visits,
But I wash,
And eat soup,
And I pray.

Before long,
The guests will come.
They won't notice that I am
Still the elder,
Who washed and waited,
Who ate and prayed
Alone.

Instead,
They'll bring potluck dishes
And bottles of wine.
They'll know that I know,
That they thank me.

They'll pour the wine,
And raise the toast,
"To health!"
And so we'll eat and drink
And then I'll say, "Come with me,
Let's all dance in the street."

Loretta Tobin

Applause *(Madrid, March 2020)*

The ravine walls of opposite blocks
open to life: faces, hands of unknown neighbors
spring from nests, homes made monastic cells,
rooms we've been sent to for quiet time,

and from each sealed-off existence
unite in applause for doctors, nurses, orderlies,
for ambulances racing up the avenue below,
for med students pressed into service
before an avalanche of suffering,
the advancing wall of death
we ask them to hold back from us.

The whistles, shouts, *¡Bravos!, ¡Vivas!,* rise
into the deep blue auditorium of evening
where Venus and a sliver of moon
gaze bright and blank at us,
transient inhabitants of their fellow planet.

I want the applause to reach them,
wake these dead worlds' ears
to what they miss by being stones,
the desperate tragic beauty we've risen to,
the hope that is our lifeblood,

a small flame blazing audacious
before the indifference of night.

Cary Barney

Field Notes from More Than Likely COVID19

My friends' texts pop up like crocuses
heralding not spring but past roots.
How are you today? How are you feeling? Need anything?
How are you feeling today? What's the Catie report?
I can bring you something if you need something...

What are your plans for the pandemic lockdown
I ask. "Working on the house, eating right, cooking beans,
never bathing." "We might wind up with a clean house
and a tidy yard." "Helping my kid pass 11th grade."
"For reasons of domestic peace I need to figure out that weed thing."

My therapist (by phone) grants me permission
to be glad it's spring. It's the second day of spring, in fact,
and I've just started to feel
not as bad.

My realtor wants to know if I've gotten tested.
There are no tests.
He knows this.
But if I had gotten a test
his family could get a test.
There are no tests. Well, there is a test,
but its lack has spread exponentially.

The good spirits stage.
The Eyeore stage.
The bored stage.
The bored stage.
The bored stage.

The stages are blank without actors, musicians, please
let them return as spring does.

I open the balcony door
and let the air in.
It's too cold, but it's fresh.

Catherine Bull

Life in the Time of Coronavirus

How strange to awake to the singing robins, to stay
in bed without worry of being late, to enjoy breakfast
in the backyard, the pool waterfall cascading over rocks
the only sound breaking the morning silence.

How strange to cook before lunch and eat in the kitchen
with my husband and son—a salad, an entrée, a dessert. No
more pre-cooked food in the office, re-warmed in the microwave,
gulped down while I answer emails and keep track of time so as
not to be late for my next class.

How strange not having to drive or pay for gas every week. My
SUV must be thankful for its break from the burning sun of the
College parking lot, the melting of its plastic parts, from the heat
that makes it gasp when I start its engine for the way back to our
cool garage. The roaring roads are quiet; the sky shows off its
bluest hue, and a cleaner wind blows by the scudding clouds.

How strange to continue life despite all that is happening—turn
work and school online, enjoy time with the family, walk out
the dog, exercise—while thousands of people are dying each day,
alone, neglected, and untreated, while companies and businesses
are closing, discharging workers who cannot sustain their families,
all without certainty of the prevention and time span of this pandemic,
as if we were unhuman, not vulnerable, scared.

How strange to still be untouched by a virus that lurks everywhere,
awaiting the moment it will prey on my family, my friends, and me.

Mari-Carmen Marin

Prison Life

My Bedroom -
was always my safe
sanctuary.
A quiet place to relax after work,
A place to watch tv or read a book,
Where I laid my head and slept every night.

My Bedroom -
now holds back the
germs.
An unseen virus that could attack me,
My family quarantined in other rooms,
The loneliness too much to stand sometimes.

My Bedroom -
has now become
walls that begin to close in
and suffocate me.
My sanctuary becomes my prison.
But I know this prison will save my life.

Kayla Matheson

Podcast

3/20/20

We had to pack up most of our home. Unfortunately I can't say why. Then we had to make the extremely difficult decision of whether to stay in our home or not, while fighting the clock on New York's lockdown last week. Deciding how to get a car into the city.
How to get the kids out. If we would be able to fill prescriptions for Luke. If gas stations were open. If we would be able to get food. If hospitals were overbooked where we were going. If my mental health would be ok. If the kids would be ok.
Money
Jobs
Kids school
Therapy
ABA
Speech
Everything that everyone is experiencing right now.

3/27/20

Officially done with week one of this new normal. Just finished putting the kids to bed. I sat down and looked at the blocks. They had managed to glue themselves to the floor this entire week, but we did it. We had somehow just accomplished a week off school for a fifth and first grader, including occupational and speech therapy. Plus being a full time student and Jason has a full time job. From the time we woke up to the time we went to bed we worked our asses off.

I was going to drop out of school so that I could focus on taking care of my family through this time, but then I realized I wouldn't have health insurance. Isn't that crazy? I am now forced to keep a position as a full time student in order to maintain my health insurance during a global pandemic. Luckily, at the beginning of the week I signed a petition at Marymount Manhattan to make all classes a pass/fail instead of receiving letter grades for this semester. This was a success and it is now being offered at the college.

I am trying to keep the kids mentally, physically, and emotionally, healthy. I am trying to be real with my feelings but shelter them from fear. For example, Luke told me he wanted to go home and he missed our fish, Myer. last night as we were brushing his teeth. I could not do anything but just nod and say "me too buddy, this is soooo hard being away from home".
Kids are resilient. They wake up everyday with a fresh sense of newness and peace.

For The Observer

As for creating, I spent my last night in New York painting a large 60x72 inch canvas. I told myself I had to paint before I packed regardless of the time. Fiery reds, lucid yellows, I was so angry. I was mad at everything, everyone, and every particle of space that was breathing. I felt trapped in earth for the first time.

Look at how we treat ourselves. I fear that this is a consequence of our selfish extractions.

I was mad that I could not feel any instincts on how to treat the situation. Making decisions for yourself is hard but making decisions for a family is terrifying. The responsibility is so powerful. Motherhood is so powerful.
{I have attached photos of this work}
We are taking it day by day. We are figuring it out. We are figuring out a lot about ourselves.
I am so thankful for life. The virus, the lock down, the isolation…. It makes me want to hug my family and never let go. So many emotions.

Blakelee Harmon

The Hunkering Down

The morning light is odd, the sky
a stranger, one could easily
fall in love with,
just as easily kill for.
That light is a liar, and like
most liars, lovely.
The mountains smoke their last, wait for
hikers, tornadoes, zombies, butterflies in love.
Like most once-pretty women, I wonder
how well I will wear this end of days.
With, one would hope, clean undies,
perfect brows, and my best
sardonic adverbs. This is
not the time, dear neighbors, for 911 calls

on dog turds, public belching, or
off-schedule moons. This is the time
to wage a blind kindness, to offer a token
to the strangers next door.
The simplest things are now
precious as gemstones, no least facet
taken for granted. The fluffy cumulus clouds
we dispense from the toilet paper roll
are rationed at least in half. Our houses,
worn like snail shells by anxious mothers,
are bleached beyond white.
We cook more, cough less.
We play cards, post videos, fill windows
with glittery hopeful stars.
We wipe all evidence of ourselves
from tables and doorknobs.
We park our shoes on the porch.
Each room has its elephant now.
The unspoken roars.

We slip into the white space, not enough
words to anchor us.
Ours is a
softer apocalypse, families walking into sunsets
and away from the caves where
we've cached our lives.
We can only grieve in increments,
swaddle our denial like colicky babies. Our hands,
kindling dry, talk for us now, our lungs
full of assassins. We reacquaint ourselves
with the sky, while scrubbing off our warren stink.

The sky, lovely bauble, has the nerve to
pirouette like a prima, as though all is well.
The sky, unlike us,
can run away.

Laura Saint Martin

Click

I check the news (a click of automation),
laptop mounted before my sallow face.
The world prepared us for this isolation.

Teenagers text from hot beds of hibernation,
burrow under covers, grip their phone's slick case.
They check the news (a click of automation).

Lovers stroke their screens regardless of location,
forget the feel of goose-bumped skin on lace.
The world prepared them for this isolation,

for flat bodies flushed with computation
that hunger for a virtual embrace.
I check the news. A click of automation

shows violinists wilting without invitation
to perform. A cellist croons to empty space.
The world prepared us all for isolation

with blue light that seeps into generations
of spellbound children, parents, glued in place.
So we check the news—a click of automation
that prepared us for this isolation.

Sophie Scolnik-Brower

When Screens Replace Touch

Invisibility I say when my son asks
what superhero power I would choose.

I wasn't much older than he is when I set
my goal to being a disembodied spirit.

Think I'll have that one day because I'm lucky.
I'd forego touch if I could go unseen, but I'd rather

have it all — the feel of wind and fingertips,
skin and hair and be out of sight.

Fond of woods, yurts, and tents for their
simple beauty it's true, but also their lack

of mirrors. I don't perceive a movie of me when
we talk, which is why it scares me when you ask

*Why do you look like that? Why did you make
that face?* How do I know? I can't see me.

A man once responded only
to my words, he held still to my

hand through grimace, shrug, even tear never
asking. I tag him the one that got away.

Can't faces be just about the rest — breath,
blinks, kisses, sustenance, and not freckles and

wrinkles, pretty eyes and cute noses, crooked
teeth and dark circles.

Yet here we are. You watching me, and me watching
me and I don't know where else to look.
me and I don't know where else to look.

Kristin Ferragu

Inside and Outside

Inside, days are a blur
Bleeding into one another
Piles of dishes that constantly reappear
Hair in a messy bun for weeks
Counting down the seconds until naptime then bedtime
Numbing ourselves with TV shows, movies, games
And cookies, dozens of cookies until they're all gone

A walk every day or two to clear your head
Try and inhale some sunlight
Bring the outside into our bodies
A hot shower if you're lucky
To wash off the failure, boredom and loneliness of
yesterday
Getting dressed back into pajamas
No need for clothes or makeup

You are not what you once were out there
Inside we are quiet, we are slow
We notice the ticking of the clocks
The clicking of the keyboards
The crumbs crawling across the floor
Frustration ebbs and flows
Then everything stands still

Outside, I come alive again
The only place that still seems normal
The trees that have stood for eternity
Will continue on long after we're gone
The air, the sky, the grass, just as we left it
Until I see the red plastic tape snaking
Around the playgrounds

Even the outside has changed now
We've all changed, inside and outside

Felicia Zuniga

Inside Out

The box
I'm in
of faces four
mentality behind
closed doors

No sickness
lurking here,
except for
loneliness,
and **Fear**

Germs our bodies
mean to fight
immunity strong,
community gone,
we belong
together

Yet freedom's lost
demand the reasons
for such a cost
such grave a season,
and questions surge

We were behaving
not raving

not ranting
'free us now'
you'll hear
our chanting

From lawlessness
which binds the time
from secrets
that pervade
our minds

To hearts that work
to heal mankind
with sonnet, dance,
and songs,

A smile
to lift us up
to gift us hope
for health
and humankind

For peace and joy
yes hope, at least
for **all** to find
beyond the COVID-1&9

Hannah K Walizer Cook

Looking Outside

at the empty streets and the hallowed lanes stripped of the
faces and the laughter, the cheers dying in the fading noise

there is more to this silence than the darkness stuck
in the black teeth of the night

the thrumming of the lone harp wire falling on the empty ears
the rolling of the subways bouncing off the empty walls

Silence screams the loudest cleaving the hunger in our souls
the pixelated appearance of the gentle soft faces on the screen

a metaphor for social company. A replacement for warm breaths
on the back of my neck for that phantom apricity

the waves throbbing and breaking on the empty shores returns
half-hearted to the places

not baptized by the fleeting touch of the soft palms
and baby fat legs dipped for mere excitement

giggles lost in the pulverized sands as the barren beach
calls out for mercy, this deafening silence is no longer pristine and pure

social distancing is the pure sustenance we all are craving these days
we now look with our parched eyes to foil the gaps in our sight

which we slowly brought on ourselves living in this orphan moment
as the corrupt architect of this empty world.

Megha Sood

Make an Effort, Make Your Bed

Don't sweat the big stuff,
And it's mostly all big stuff big scary stuff.
Sweat the small stuff instead
for self sanity's sake
find dignity in the discipline
of doing the small stuff.

Make an effort, make your bed,
brush your teeth, comb your hair,
shit, shower and shave.
Get dressed, get rest,
eat right, meditate, do downward dog
and clean up after yourself.

Wash the dishes, wash your clothes.
Read, write, listen, learn.
Be kind be calm.
Comfort, family friends and neighbors.
Limit exposure to orange-faced grifter's jibber-jabber.

Don't sweat the big stuff, it's mostly all
big stuff, too goddamn big, scary stuff.
Sweat the small stuff
honor the small stuff by sweating *it*.
The small stuff we can handle.
The small stuff is all we've really got.

Robert Eugene Rubino

#selfcareinthetimeofcorona

I got out of bed today
        so the floor wouldn't be lonely.
Put on my favorite sweater
        so it wouldn't forget my scent.
Brushed my hair
        to add a few more strands for the brush to count.
Flirted with make-up
        so they'd stay loyal and forgive my flaws.
Put on my shoes
        so their souls recall the shape of my feet.

Mysti Frost

Backpacks

The Bermuda grass falls out
in bits and pieces like hair.
It's not a garden, it's a sphere.
Inside the ball, there is a family.
Outside the ball, there is a family.

In the vast yard, there is chalk
and thoughts and thoughts of
alcohol and thoughts and
thoughts of leaving and
thoughts about the source of
this infection [patient zero].
The street lights still work.
People still like to run the red.
La vecina still pokes at my ease.

Swinging like an artist,
is another peach hibiscus
rubbing at a bald spot in the grass.
It's itchy I presume.
Will we aim for the coastline,
with backpacks full of
powdered milk and sanitizers?
Will we leave our home?

Nicole Hospital-Medina

Day 16 of Quarantine: Breathe

No matter how late I wake up I still make breakfast .
Today, flaxen oats bubble with cinnamon and brown sugar
And I remember my innocence and wonder
If I'll ever wake up to a morning in which I am called "Mama."

The pour over finishes dripping and I
Stare down into my reflection on russet liquid
I breathe in the French Roast aroma like a prayer
How can healing prevail in desolation?

Outside the kitchen window
I see a robin dancing in a rain puddle and
For a moment I forget how many people are dying
For a moment I forget nobody knows what's coming next
For a moment I am concerned with nothing but this robin
Who is doing the same thing robins always do in April

I step outside to the front patio where the sun is gleaming
In shades of light worth cherishing
It soaks into my shoulders
The way the sun always does

I hear the echo of children's joys
Over their respective backyard fences
It reminds me of the feeling in my heart
When I, too, believed this world could keep me safe

There are some things that are strong enough
To stop the world in its tracks
And yet still, the robins dance
The sun gleams, the children play
The blare of global pandemic is deafening, but the
reverberation of faith is louder still

While every breath feels heavy with uncertainty and loss
The goodness we still have is the remedy to free our chests
I smile down into my reflection on russet liquid
And breathe it all
In

Syble Heffernan

Eleven Days: Living Under a 21st Century Pandemic

March 18: New Mexico closes restaurants and bars. The brewery manager at Second Street will fill our growler before sending us home.

He has fired 110 people today and it is only noon.

March 19: Yogis convene through computer screens on living room floors. Thousands tune into webinars. I meet my dog trainer via zoom.

Shame is out the window, trashy TV is in.

March 20: Weekdays fade into weekends with little distinction. The ski hill is closed, churches are too.

No one is brunching.

March 21: I call my mother-in-law and sing happy birthday. She responds with charming deep laughter.

"I'm more emotional today than usual." She meets her church group via zoom.

March 22: The usps driver arrives late tonight, the sky is near-dark. I wonder how many hands have touched the mail I do not want before it will reach my own.

Does he wear gloves?

March 23: 6 feet. 50 shoppers. 69,000 cases. 14 days. 2 trillion dollars. 3 bodies. 1 house.

March 24: I visit the dog park every few hours to remember what it feels like to hear other people speak, to watch other bodies in action. There, I walk the high ridge as if it were my own. Hugged by mountains on all sides, I am blanketed by the big sky.

In the presence of beauty, loneliness fades.

March 25: My brother schedules a birthday event through zoom. My partner and I wear party hats I made from scrapbook paper when we join the party, huddled around my laptop at the table.

I wonder if *zoom* will become the word for meeting, like google has for search.

March 26: Strangers shy away. An older woman four feet from me kindly asks me to move—she gingerly selects three avocados. An older man, less tender, cries, "six feet!" when I unconsciously step forward, closer to him.

I'm surprised by how the distance hurts.
March 27: My friend has the Covid. She goes out every three days to get kale for her rabbit. I don't understand why this is necessary, but I don't say that.

Not now.

March 28: We kick sand onto our yoga mats, laugh and strain to hear the instructor's voice from my iPhone over the steady hum of traffic above the dry river bed where we practice.

Beneath blue skies in the presence of a friend, I forget to fear.

Alyssa Kreikemeier

Once More

Dark circles under my mother's eyes
Have deepened as Dad drives away,
Leaving to see patients at the hospital again
Without the necessary protection
She fears he may become one, too

Once empty nesters, their house now filled
With me and my brothers
Mandatory evacuations from school
Have brought us back to childhood bedrooms

All aspects of life are changing
Screen to screen, I meet my friends
Still hard to hear their voice behind
Pixelated noise and spotty connections

Once a day I step outside
To see cherry blossoms still in bloom
But these days I travel window to window
Wondering, waiting, nearly
Angry whenever a plane flies over

When did something as simple as
A handshake between neighbors, a hug
An embrace between old friends
Become so deadly?

We were not made to be alone
Dare to dream of a world we can
Reunite without fear. But for now,
I hear the sound of my brothers' laughter,
Mom singing in the kitchen,
My dad coming home,
Walking through the door once more

Anna Delamerced

Stuck in the Funhouse

walls of glass
reflections of fluorescent rods
flickering yellow, white, red

hallways that press in
on mirrors of shoulders
dead end shoes

I can see woods
clearly make out
the world growing spring

but here in this boxcar maze
I pace pathways
like a lion on cement

heavy, tired, and sick
from constant clowns
laughing from hidden wires

eventually slump
against a pane
I cannot escape

Eric Machin Howd

3
Virus

61

Adrenalin Rush

Before our fears hovered on every face
(when we were brave enough to step outside),
I am trying to remember what it was like
to hug someone, to reach out for a hand.

When we were brave enough to step outside,
strangers stepped away. Even if they wanted
to hug someone, to reach out for a hand,
we all knew that distance was required.

Strangers stepped away even if they wanted
to save our souls or talk about blessed days.
We all knew that distance was required.
Our desire for so much more was ravenous.

To save our souls or talk about blessed days,
how we ached for contact, revered its rush.
Our desire for so much more was ravenous –
how our cortex lit up like a candelabra!

How we ached for contact, revered its rush!
Someone needs to look back at what we craved –
how our cortex lit up like a candelabra –
at the memory of touching each other.

Someone needs to look back at what we craved:
the tantalizing thrill of adrenaline
at the memory of touching each other
before our fears hovered on every face.

Mary O'Melvany

Seduction by Virus

Yes, you might say, I'm a little obsessed.
But, please, let me shelter in your warm
breath over this cold, gray, winter day. I can't
help but want closeness with you. Oh,
how I yearn to be taken
inside. Press me against your face,
suck my essence from your wind-
chapped lips. Or lick me, Honey,
off your fingertips. I tire of being an exiled ghost
beneath the lens of a microscope. Make me
real, make me *seen*. I promise I'll take my time
with you. Maybe, I'll never leave. You are mine
and while I am here, there is no other.
I love how your skin glistens in my damp
excitement, this clammy calamity. You
must know that you are all I have
ever wanted, your weakness and heat
spells my reason to live. Let me spread
over all of you, to multiply my kisses, expanding
within your moist darkness. Let me turn in spirals
around your tongue, and drip my love
down your throat, to inhale your air, to fold
deep into your flesh. We will be one, my Love.
Give in to my spinning hot fevers, my shivery
chills running salt-sweat down your spine.
Baby, I can taste you from here and I want to
take your breath away. I want to possess
your blood, muscle and bone. Let me take
you in this erotic demise, and we will both
go down together. Cancel all your plans:
you're home
alone, with me,
for the duration.

Julia Gordon-Bramer

Exposed

Old office phone, the incessant bell,
The shrillness shocked my ears.
Delicate information, a warning of status.
Loud, clear, and on full alarm. Worst fears –

You've been exposed.

A handshake, a common courtesy,
It wasn't across the world anymore.
Counting backwards to the last exchange,
Churning, curling, boiling within my core.

I've been exposed.

Smallest sneeze, birthing my anxieties,
Hiking ever higher to peaks of accentuation.
Guilt gnawing at every step I've taken:
Each purchase, kiss, and conversation.

He's been exposed.

A link in the chain, deemed essential.
After ten days, put back on the front lines,
Witnessing the collective pain of the looming fight:
Recession, headlines, and crowded minds.

They've been exposed.

Kisses blown through barriers, generations kept apart,
but a defense is forged on an intangible frontier.
The cloud begins to lift, a network called to aid.
Education, work, and community: The future is here.

We've been exposed.

Amelia Bostic

In Today's News

And the news comes on
Somewhere in the background
The national station, with serious voices.

"Mammy, I can't figure out this maths question"
"Where's my pencil? MAM! He took my pencil."

And the news rumbles on, half my ear upon it
Ten people died today
Yesterday
There were only 3
Only 3 people gone, 3 families grieving
Today it is ten.
Tomorrow it will be more.

"Mam, the radio said dead." My 6 year old is solemn
"They said dead, I don't like that."

And the news continues,
There are nearly two thousand cases
The median age for death is over 70
The clusters are in nursing homes

MY 89 year old mother glances at me
I thank all my gods that she's home

"I still can't do the maths question!"
"He won't give back my pen."

And half my eye upon them, half on my computer screen
Working from home, home now a school
My living room a sea of papers, washing, books,
I listen to the news.

Geraldine Moorkens Byrne

Cosmic Awareness

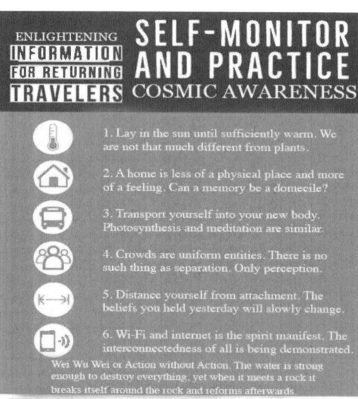

Benjamin Champagne

The Thing with No Form

How is it that something intangible can bind us, trap us,
keep us prisoner?

It has no form, and yet it overpowers us, it entangles us,
and seeps into our lives.

We look back sometimes, completely powerless to where
it has taken us, what damage it has done.

And there seems like no way out from the power
and destruction of the thing with no form.

And no one knows that it's there, except us.

It grips at the lives of our people.

Some are wounded in a deep, deep place that they don't even know
about yet. It is utter fear to even put words to it.

And uncapping this terror would be like containing a tidal wave.

There is just no way to face it without it becoming all we can see.

How can we possibly make it through?

The moment our heart can see our hand in someone else's pain, we
are burdened with the truth that there is no turning back.

We cannot change what's been done.
We cannot undo it.

We wish beyond anything in this life to undo it, but there is no
stopping time.

Nicole Williams

Corona Pantoum

Man in a blue face mask
protected from the pandemic
that hasn't even arrived yet.
Now suddenly there's a crowd,

protected from the pandemic,
all of them in blue face masks.
Now suddenly there's a crowd
like a flock of jittering birds

all of them in blue face masks--
a species characteristic,
a flock of jittering birds
alive in future transparent.

A species characteristic:
they can foresee disaster
alive in future transparent.
H-Mart's a hospital

where they flock, foresee disaster
as they pluck pomelos and plums.
The street is a hospital,
and I'm an ignorant fool.

They pluck pomelos and plums
this place, suffused with the virus,
and we are innocent fools
breathing as if it's still air.

The air's suffused with a virus
that hasn't even arrived yet.
We breathe as if it's just air.
There's a man in a blue face mask.

Monica Raymond

Bubbles in a War Zone …

It takes time to feel comfortable in a war zone -
At 8 pm your family clap, holler hope, give thanks
I take a 5 minute break, coffee (lots) and doughnuts.
My hands crack from their thousand-a-day scrubs
I cool you, drain you, cleanse you, oxygenate your
lungs, lesions from beautiful microscopic aliens
A tornado of experts keep you here, flatten this curve
I'm raw with sores behind my ears from mask elastic
cuts. Stitch groups make headbands with big buttons,
and builders send PPE, their protection in demolition.
Your ventilation soundtracks, breath shunts and beeps
I'm practiced not 'hardy', cry briefly as beds fall empty,
staff share an inappropriate joke and my smile is back.
In the next bed, a sister – mild asthma, a dad – angina,
a mum – diabetic, a youngster misses playing football.
I find a vial in my coat pocket given instead of confetti
at a wedding. I blow bubbles at the end of tough shifts.
We meet in this pandemic together, intimate strangers.
Tonight we stay back, share donated prosecco, order
takeaways paid for in kind, and tomorrow I will sleep.

Helen Sheppard

What if

What if the nurse weighs you, leaves you standing in
stocking feet, says she feels sick and has to go home,
and your neighbor is diabetic and you dare not look into
her isolated eyes; what if your fridge drips and your
meat rots but no repairman will enter your house
and you've not heard another's voice bounce off your
antiseptic walls nor a hello sift through the screen door;
what if you evade the coughing shopper and find out
your dearest friend next door is among the infected;
what if your daughter is distraught three thousand miles
away from where you wait behind locked doors, afraid
the virus could lay siege to your old lungs; and your son
is out of work and needs to raid his inheritance before
you have a chance to die?

But all the what-ifs go unanswered once the barrel
takes you down the rapids of that broken-bone feeling,
that furiously shivering fever that has you wheezing and
begging to leave you dead or alive.

Krista Lubatkin

To A Plague Rat

I've watched you walking, as you wished
As you've crept with toxic step
From stone to sea to shore

From stone to sea to shore you've slipped
A flash of fur, a saboteur
Your skin unscoured, unshorn

Your skin, unscoured, unshorn, is stained
With vanity, rose red, pretty
As bright as bone and blood

Bright as bone and blood, you boast
In flashbulb flare your vermin's hair
A smile as sure as sin

A smile as sure as sin shelters
The waiting death, the final breath
A promised peal of plague

A promised peal of plague, a drop
Of poison spun of pride, of one
Whose worth outweighs the world

Whose worth outweighs the world, willing
To salt the fields and taint their yields
Long as your life's still led

Long as your life's still led, you'll lay
A funeral shawl that thwarts the call
For care; your care is caustic

Justin Moir

Intubed

"I will talk as a friend."
Weber spoke dirge to empty darkness.
The Ukrainian woman asked to bring
her husband back from the dead,
over and over and over until
nothing more to inhale and exhale.
"That night I cried," He said.
What did he say? He say?
Day in, day out seven days.
Day out, day in seven days.

At night I tossed and turned.
She was still, straight still, still.
No toss and turn for her.
No finger gripped an empty night.
Feet tied tight against hard board.
That night I tossed and turned.
Her eyes whish right, whish left,
No toss and turn for her.
Inhale, exhale, inhale, exhale, whish, brish
Blink, blink, up, down, blink, breathe.
Whish in, brish out, Whish in
Sleep, eyes closed, awake and blink.
Today lay straight as a pin.
 Lay straight to hope, to hope,
or else, or else, or else.

Night nine, blue room, blue scrubs.
Doctor Blue with empty hands outstretched,
"It's time, no waiting, wait's gone."
Choose breath, choose tracheotomy, choose
death.
No time to pound, pound, pound,
the heart chest bound. I robot
whisper, "I love you." Hearts, pound,
pound alone, alone, "Jesus loves you.
"Blue nurse says, "Go, go now."
Outside Blue curtains I grip Formica.
What did Weber say about Blue?
Was the Ukrainian woman really Blue?

Richard Glen Smith

During My Illness

I had a glimpse, for a split second,
of the world carrying on without me.
The trees keep growing. The sun
keeps burning in the sky. Waves
continue lapping at the stony shores.
Folks go on attending universities,
working in bakeries and drugstores
and restaurants. Gardens grow,
go fallow and grow again. Lovers climb
into cars and drive places. They push
the button on the gas pump and fill their tanks.
They drive to the grocery store, choose
between organic and non-organic avocados.
Children dangle their feet in cool water
while their parents lift cameras to capture
their silhouettes against the setting sun.
I saw that I was small. I was the size of a piece of dust.
I was but a sparrow that lands, sings, and is forgotten.

Kim June Johnson

Intubation

I wake in purgatory, where I hear
The rhythmic ventilator's pulse and see
My hands and feet restrained. There seems to be
No way to flee paralysis and fear.
Intensive care, a cell with pale green walls,
Imprisons me, a soul without a voice,
Immobile, intubated, lacking choice.
The ventilator's soft whish lifts and falls.
Outside this hospital the city fears
Contagion, deprivation, even death,
And many conversations end in tears.
But I am now reduced to breath, then breath.
No other act is possible. I weep
In silent isolation. Then I sleep.

Sara Cupp Smith

A Pandemic Day

It feels
like tunneling
through
a tube
of tidal slime,
an insulated
secluded
climb
ascending
to a bilious end
where horizons
abduct
essential
light,
punctuating
a silent
night.

Barbara Reynolds

Then the World Changed

A spreader used to be a lorry that made roads safe in winter.
Social isolation used to be practiced by those with
agoraphobia.
A transmission used to be something you heard on the radio.
Incubation used to be reserved for premature babies
A virus used to be a thing you didn't want on your computer.

Then the world changed.

How the world changed.

Henry Bladon

Pandemic
(we are many)

we stop asking where
all the good meat goes

or what they have
or what we don't

one pot cooks rice
for the whole family

the cart still needs
to be pulled

we do what we can
what we should

and on the night
of the coldest winds
we are many
while they are few

Anne Carly Abad

Pandemic
(I Hear My Father's Voice)

What I think of
are the stories of my mother and father.

My father,
turning off all the unused lights
that my sister and I had left on.
My mother,
stocking canned goods on the pantry shelves.
My father,
taking the leftovers from our plates,
"Give it here, I'll finish it."

Both of them,
remembering a time
when there was not enough.
Born in the early part of the last century,
living through World War I,
the Great Depression,
ration cards through WWII.

As children,
did my parents have
indoor plumbing?

Was toilet paper a luxury?
Or were the pages
of the Sears Roebucks in use?
There were mentions of corn cobs
And other substitutes.

I hear my father's voice
saying more than once,
        "You don't know how good
        you've got it."
He's right.
The Depression saw breadlines
        on almost every block.
Toilet paper was not as important
        As food,
        keeping the electricity on,
        paying the rent.
Starvation and despair were commonplace.

There is one thing though,
        they did have
        that we cannot have now.

Human Touch.

A hug from a grandmother,
        a visit from an aunty, cousins,
        uncles.
Gatherings of large and small
        families.
Sitting on the front porch
        with neighbors.

Having face to face conversations
        With friends.
Sharing meals,
dancing cheek to cheek,
singing in choirs or just a duet.

Hopefully, this virus
will not take too many lives.
Hopefully, this isolation
will not scare us
from hugging friends once more,
when we can.

Hopefully, when this ends –
        and it will –
        we will remember
        what it's like to be together.
        And we will cherish that.

And we won't give a damn
about toilet paper

Barbara Schwegman

Rights

Native or immigrant, your barbed wire
camps and guards can't contain me. Don't
you understand? My whole life is a fight.
I want what anyone wants: safety and a place
where I can root in and call home,
a source to sustain me, and someone
to latch onto and love in this short life.
I seek your freedoms—to cross
borders, to be with who I want,
to procreate without judgment, to be all
I am capable of being.
Is it my fault that I was born
into suffering, and that misery
really does love company?
I am not responsible for your lack
of immunity. Don't blame me
because I'm popular with the elderly;
we sing songs from the 50s and 60s
some go as far back as 1918.

Think of me as a lost traveler, a refugee
seeking asylum. Consider me
an adventurer exploring land and sea. And you
study my culture, a spiky orb
expanding across the globe,
globbing up the petri dish. My history
is nonexistent. My ancestry was conjured
new in a witch's brew of bat
wings and rat fleas. They say Asia.
But perhaps, I evolved out of the deep
Congo or settled first in South or Central
America. I move
across nations by breath and touch,
a sneeze and fever dreams.
You plan the extermination of my kind.
You call me virus. I call you my
Louisiana Purchase.

Julia Gordon-Bramer

Black Swan Song

I have killed my millions
And feel no sorrow

While you superior creatures
Weep

I am always here
Waiting for a crack in hygiene
A lapse in consumerism
Fuelled by traditional belief in "jinbu":
   Fill the void, find a cure,
   With black market wildlife "qi"

I am not the rarest
   But ravenous

While I am wild
   Outside
   Making contact

You retreat,
Superior ones

You have found my genome
   In time for next Chinese New Year

Pam Fox

What is Left

I couldn't breathe right
for a while.
It wasn't that I was trapped in my bedroom,
quarantined,
that scared me.
It was that I forgot
what spaciousness
in my lungs
felt like.

When I recovered
I began to see space
where it wasn't before.
My furniture began disappearing.
Items I had collected and loved
became the negative
spaces
between emptiness
which is really
openness.

I began to see through my walls
like windows.
The ground
disappeared
under my feet.

I realized that people, too,
are places
where spaces
could be.

And what I mostly need
is me.

Kat Milberger

4
Wry

89

Shop-fever
(after John Masefield)

I must go down to the shops again, to a supermarket, close by,
and all I ask is a smallish queue and a bouncer six foot high,
no young or old queuing in the cold, no carrier bags shaking,
nor a grey mist on the car park's face, nor a grey dawn breaking.

I must go down to the shops again, to the cleaning products aisle
where the hand gel has arrived again, I'm hearing all the while,
and all I have is a facial mask, a two-metre gap applying,
plus the averted glance of the wide berth dance, as we're panic buying.

I must go down to the shops again, and not keep putting it off,
but I feel the knotted stomach and fear the virulent cough,
and all I ask is some fennel stalks and vacuum-packed red clover,
and the restocked shelves of our former selves when the lockdown's over.

Mike Dunne

Pretend You're a Dangerous Dissident

Got the coronavirus
shelter-in-place social-distancing
make-America-greedy-speedy-again
full-of-bluster blues?

Pretend you're
a celebrity leaker of secrets and screeds
under house arrest
or solitary Mandela stuck on Robben Island

or Rasputin the mad mystical monk
marooned in a Czarist monastery
or Thelonious Monk holed up in Harlem
mulling deep mysterious musical thoughts.

Pretend you're
a dangerous dissident (a democratic socialist,
perhaps!)
hunkering down hiding out
in a Silicon Valley safe house

waiting for the cool clear day
when all the parched people
call upon you — you of all people —
to slake their raw raspy-throated thirst.

Robert Eugene Rubino

Leaves Me Breathless

Covid.
Weighs in the mouth like a human name.
"Did you hear the news about Covid?"
"Covid's been getting around."

"Ugh, I hate Covid."

19 is Covid's last name, but me and Covid are on a
first-name basis.
Friends? No, of course not.
It doesn't even know I exist yet,
But I've been obsessing over it for weeks
Like an 18-year-old distracted by a crush.
I know it's bad for me, but I can't stop.
I stalk it on social media,
Peeking at who it's been seeing,
Hoping it picks me over my friends,
Trying my best to keep my parents from meeting it.

Covid.
Weighs nothing, yet sits heavy,
Pressing the air from gasping chests.

Serial killer shows have been popular
among women my age.
Dangerous is sexy.
But not like this. This is not what we meant.

I get dolled up in my daytime pyjamas,
Pour a glass of wine,
And refresh, to see what Covid's up to.

Roisin Boyle

troubadours of the scaffold

two steel poles   balanced on his shoulder as he climbs the ladder

baseball cap askance
beard, a half-life growth
trainers, a muddy, scuffed comfort

maybe he speaks in tongues
a cuss riddled merge of verb, noun, and adjective

"business as usual" loudly sung
as he and his fellows up atop the roof   admire the skyline

while others quarantine   their world goes on   even as ours has stopped

Trevor Maynard

Which Way is Up?

Don't want to get up,
Don't want to lie down.
Don't want to be maudlin,
Don't want to play clown.

Don't want to go out,
Don't want to stay in.
I guess just like me,
This old life's wearin' thin.

. . . So I'll let the dogs in,
and cue up the booze,
then kill the time strummin'
some Rhythm'n' Blues ... .

Tonia Kalouria

The Lilac Bush

We ripped out the lilac bush. It sat next to the shed that held the water heater, the ancient boiler, the circuit breaker that popped whenever we used that one outlet in the living room. We demolished the shed to expand the house, and the lilac bush went with it. The lilac bush that would be in bloom right now if it were still here, but it isn't. The lilac bush that the dog would be sleeping beneath, flowers branching out above his head like purple sun rays beaming from an auburn core, but the dog is gone now too. Gone even before the lilac bush, though I still picture him daily, an apparition moving through the house, including the new rooms, spaces he never inhabited.

In winter, when the lilac would have been barren, spindly, the new walls went up. The spot where it once stood now looks like a place where a lilac had never been, would never grow. I told my husband that I'd feel a bit sad come spring, our first without the lilac.

I didn't know how much the world would change by the time spring arrived, the lilac bush the least of

the things we have lost.

Claire Taylor

(a version of this poem was previously published in Capsule Stories, 2020)

Cyanthropic Daze

We have all become our dogs it seems,
Stirring at first light
To these Groundhog Day mornings,

All is the same and all is different

So eager for that first walk
The chance of possibility,
We sniff the fecund smells
Of earth, stream
Moss,
We give tree-distance to the squirrel
And air rights to the hawk,

Then to the car,
A ride! *I call shotgun,*
The window cracked open
Just the enough to
Moisten our mature noses,
Take in a piece of wind,
The still fallow fields,

And then we return home,
There it is:
The couch,
Where we can circle our
Perfect spot, to stretch,
To dream perhaps
Of blissful playdates,
And under our
Breaths,
Bark at the
Baleful world

Peter Bruno

The end of the world from the inside of the house

I fish the world out of my pocket
and notice that it's dying.
Behind my six-digit passcode
the apocalypse awaits. A pale horse, neon rider.
I scroll through until I get to the hope.

Put it away! Be mindful
of a world that's slipping away,
a memory seen out the window
of a spring that could've been.
On excursions I keep six feet away from the future.

Time is interesting, these ones especially so
though they're difficult to survive
rather impossible to make a living in.
At least we get to spend a long night
together, until the morning comes
in fourteen days or so.

Kohl Neal

Covid-19 Lockdown

My cat
perched
on the windowsill
spends hours
with her nose
to the glass
just to catch
flitting wings,
the wind
dancing
fronds,
lizards
sunning on
sidewalks.

An old man
in a mask
walking his dog
sets my cat's tail
scribbling.

Now I am
a house cat.

Jane Ellen Glasser

the dishes

My kids won't load the dishwasher
It's driving me insane
And so I smash the plates instead
And walk out in the rain

The air is sweet and heady
If I could survive out here I would
A feral, lonely woman
Doing what she should

I'd build a camp from things I'd find
And make a little fire
And I'd sit there for a long, long time
Until the world expires

My bones will sink much deeper
Than the mulch and wood and peat
I'll funnel down into the depth
And try and plant a seed

And after a long silence
When the awful time has passed
I'll emerge victorious
Like a crocus, a blade of grass

The darkness will still shroud me
The fear of what has been
But when I walk back into the house
The dishes will be clean.

Emma Gibson

Shouldn't We Have Enough?

People are raining down dead in New York
Doctors in need of gear
And my invalid mom I removed from the nursing home
Asks for a mask to wear, indoors in her bed
I hand one over like a comfort blankie
She will not grasp the Kleenex situation either
Until they are gone
Still, I indulge her
After admonishing, "Use only two,"
While she chirps, "Okay!"
 merrily uses five,
And stuffs a couple extra in her bathrobe pocket.

.

Mitzi Dorton

What if My Surreal is Your Surreal?

In the private hive of a public restroom,
we scour hands over distant sinks,
echo the word that anchors my feet
walking past the novel view
of emptied lots and overnight barricade.

This week, folks from church
conducted an online version of the usual
weekly contemplative service.
Spans of collective silence interspersed
with staticky song. Each of us smiling inside
our representative squares.
We in our habitats adjusting volume,
leaning forward to better arrive.

Even if my color green
isn't your color green, there is yet green.
An essence beyond the recognizable
package of person or thing.
The garden, with its empty shepherd's hook
and last year's spent debris, waits
in a waning sponge of snow
to be freshly dug.

Micki Blenkush

Hardly an Apocalypse in Here

I know the many forms of guilt well
we're old friends
hello, excessive eating
hi there, forgotten birthdays
nice to see you, weddings skipped
how's it going, funerals missed

just the same
none of my previous dalliances prepared me for this new strain

this infectious, specific remorse of enjoying myself amidst the
chaos
doing well while the world burns

my empathy for the people who are losing their worlds
doesn't seem to count when I still wake up every morning,
drinking tea in my warmest pajamas
a criminal escaping justice, corrupt diplomat in a safe house

in Brooklyn, they prepare emergency morgues
while I read Greek myths in the bath
Italian doctors debate which patients to save
as I figure out what kind of sandwich to make for lunch
someone hugs their mother for the last time
and I'm slow dancing with the Swiffer to Benny Goodman

let me tell you again:
it's not fair, it's not fair, it's not fair

and
how often it seems
the best day of your life is someone's worst

Michael Hatchett

Battered Ego

My pet bat has the Corona virus, but she's asymptomatic.
However, bats aren't in favour right now
So she's keeping her little head down.
Hidden beneath her folded wings, she tucks her furrowed snout –
Patient zero in a world frothing to place blame.

She tells everyone that she can't infect humans
But no one's listening to facts.
She posts articles daily on social media. Headlines such as:
'Bats not to blame: intermediate host required
for human infection from SARS-CoV-2 virus.'
She writes 'We're just a natural reservoir of the disease
The Pangolins are the ones being irresponsible!
Bats are victims too!' with a picture of her
Wearing a face mask, looking mournful.
The pathos is well-intended but not well received.

'Dirty bat!'

'Goddamn bat scum!'

Angry comments flow below all of her posts.
She hangs around our bedroom, sullen
- our housemates isolating her.
We watch True Blood reruns and eat dry toast.

Sometimes she flies into fits of rage at the injustice of it all.

'Why should I have to fuckin be in here?!'

'It's the fuckin Pangolins fault!'
she squeaks, rabid with recrimination.

I gently remind her that she got close.
We all get close sometimes and that's ok.

'No! It's bullshit, he kissed me! That Pangolin kissed me!'

'But you kissed him back...'

She drops from the rafters to her phone
And begins searching through her saved videos.

'I'm gonna expose him!'

30 minutes later the world's first viral
Bat-on-Pangolin amateur porn clip is trending.

Jacky T

Prepped

(*vase rhymes with mace)

Temporary measures are in place
Just in case
In pursuant of its crime
An unseen assailment
Breaks a *vase**

Doors locked, dead bolted
Two-Zero-Two-Zero
My secret keypad code
CCTV, motion detectors
All fitted by a masked *hero*

Six feet away he stood
Sweaty, and heavily built
Playing poker with Covid
All in on the river card
But my government *on tilt*

My gun is at the ready
I've stocked up just in case
This thing goes sideways
And humanity returns
To its *base*

For fourteen days
I self-isolate
Trolling on Twitter
Disseminating the real truth
King of my Castle, I *master-hate*

I said it would come
And prepped up, just in case
See you on the other side
Slight temp, itchy cough
Got no sense of smell or *taste*

As the curve gains *pace*
More speed, less *haste*
Mankind is unkind and *base*
What a fucking *waste*
Mastering the hate
Am I such a hero
Self-isolated, I thought I was safe
Until I saw the broken *vase* —

Vox Pop Max Pax

Not a Number *(the defiant)*

Not gonna follow the *Curve*　　　　　
No more *Mathematical Modelling*
Pitching death as a confirmed *Sale*
It's Negative Thinking

IF YOU CAN YOU CAN
IF YOU CANT YOU CANT
IF YOU SAY YOU DIE YOU DIE

NO!　I YELL, NO!

Not a number, refuse to be a statistic
Do not model my data, I am not a number
In this house, in this body, in my soul

||||||||||||||||||||||||||||||||||||||||||||||||||||||||||||||||||||||||||

Conrad Spenser Clark

<u>*breathe*</u>

when the factories stop
the planet breathes …………

what kind of working will we need

when the world resumes
its previrus creed?

Anonymous

The Three Stages of Social Distancing

1. Covid-19, social distancing

2. Covid-19: economic distancing

3. Covid-19: reality

Ben Ohm

Five Directions for Surviving COVID-19

1.

Tonight, lock yourself down
and forget about any travel
over water.

2.

Tackle mental doubt with soap;
sing songs when sanitizing hands.

3.

Avoid all danger by dodging
strangers; banish dust bunnies.

4.

Every speck of dirt is a suspect.
Scrub the tub until it's surface
thins a whiter shade of pale.

5.

Pandemic medics might not
arrive, so speed read or build hope
that floats boats to Mars.

.

Susan Sanders

111

5
Art

113

Postcards We Never Sent

You said: *Let's meet in New York at 3 in the morning.*
I said: *Do we j-walk, or do we JAY WELK…*a
sandwich
of language and verses
subway tracks and
fire escapes
the smell of burnt
hot dog buns, bagels,
zip lines through trees.
Full up on wonder.

Philip Glass drives
a cab in his leathers.
Offers us a tour
into the night—
a hungry ride to see
the possibility of rich people,
this sewer full of proud
wanting.

Shall we stop the cab?
Or will he,
the composer?

Soon enough
we will meet.
Palms pressed to palms.
asking each and each
to describe the how
of love.

Susana Molinolo and Pamela Yuen-Elkerbout

Bouleversée/turned upside down

Days go by
when I lose hold of wonder,
when last night's quarrel,
fresh reported slaughters,
or news of this pandemic,
crowd out the lions and holy fools.

But then
        I'm ambushed by

bluesy words
      jazz-dancing
   down
the
     syncopated
  page,

fragile stars -
frozen lace on winter windowpanes,

a revel of nasturtiums -
oranges, scarlets, yellows,
reflected in a shining copper pot.

Nan Williamson

Space Bubbles

*"When you play music in a space -- whether it's outdoor or indoors -- it includes the space, and it plays to the space. And so, since we're all having to be at a distance from each other, it's almost like you can create a **bubble** with the music, and everyone is joined in that space." ...Jodi Beder, Mt. Ranier, MD cellist speaking from her front porch about her daily cello concerts during the time of CCOVID-19. VOA News.*

The cellist sits down in her wicker chair.
It is colored silvered white, like her hair.
It is a lazy March afternoon.
She knows an audience will soon
assemble near her porch. They wait
for her to take up her bow, to create
the magic of Bach, the Beatles, Randy
Newman, Woody Guthrie. And we
all stop to hear what normal sounds like.
We still recall when closeness did not strike
fear among us. When we could imagine
gathering at concert venues -- the passion
of community mixed with joyous sounds,
how each note could bind our deepest wounds.
She knows this lesson from the precipice
of grief where once she serenaded hospice
patients. Like a gentle lover, she cradles
her ancient instrument. This act enables
us to travel like astronauts, to escape
to celestial points of view, to reshape
our current thinking, imagine spaces
far afield, a new diaspora of places
where kindness heals us all. A bubble,
if you will, which some futurist Hubble
telescope might record. There is magic here
in this simple concert. There is no need to fear
the moment we are in, no need to deploy
defenses. We are tethered by *Ode To Joy.*

Mary O'Melveny

Blossoms

Last night I dreamed
the whole economy crashed
and I had to move back
to my hometown
and work at Subway
like I did when I was seventeen.
All night the chorus of Anna Tivel's
beautiful song played over and over
in my brain: *Anthony, I'm afraid.*
But this morning, blossoms
on the windowsill, and tea,
and a walk through greening trees
the sun splitting through.
The world, for now, soft and safe.

Kim June Johnson

#quarantineartclub

(after Carson Ellis)

Who do you love? [Assignment #8]

Because sometimes that is all we can ask

ourselves—

standing

alone—

distance measured
by a world
already having insisted on—promoted—

too much space   in between.

Perhaps we'll forget entirely

the tactile feel

of human skin—

forget to marvel at its stories—
what then?
Who will we become if we stop

tracing the lines: contour of bones, crosshatch of scars & creases.

Tucked away safely in front of screens,

      our frantic fingers

           searching

keys—

    the alert-sound of a new message
triggering
our response—conditioned—Pavlovian—

    an expanse   growing   in between.

Platforms built off-site—

                apart-from—

      interfaces,

synchronous

    yet separate, no need for physical
contact at all.
Who will we become if we keep

  amplifying the silence, turning our words into clicks and tweet-counts?

In the midst of this, task yourself with the challenge:

      find the good

    in the abysmal—

join the Quarantine Art Club,
complete
Assignment #1 first: draw

your face—its features—

 be aware of the space   in between

nose and mouth, mouth and chin,

 between fretful eyes

  searching

fretful eyes—

 like a scientist, study
 your reflection
 as objectively as you can,

  Self-Portrait   *in Isolation*,

 hashtag & share.

Next, try to locate some sense of certainty,

  find an object

 in your house—

 one that won't move: consider
 a garlic clove,
 the wine bottle you emptied last night—draw

the shape of it—its outline—

without lifting your pen or pencil   in between,

keep your eyes on the subject,
your hand
in motion—a continuous,

uncontrolled flow—

look closely—Assignment #4:

Something Free (form)   *in Isolation,*

hashtag & share.

Remind yourself how much

art is saving your life—

feed your imagination,
prepare for it
each day a hardy feast—draw

a map of anywhere—here & there, a deep

blue sea   in between,

include a compass rose, an X

marking the spot—on a separate
piece of paper,
draw your new take on treasure—

what has fast turned

obsolete—Assignment #5:

X Marks the Hand Sanitizer, N95 Masks,

the Only Full Bottle of Chardonnay,

A Treasure Map of Day Twelve   in Isolation,

hashtag & share.

Who will we become after weeks

of sheltering in place? Will we be our best selves—

husband   & wife

& two dogs on the sofa,

side by side—ants breaching

the perimeter,

marching along the kitchen windowsill—
upstairs,
in the eaves of the attic, unaware

of social   distancing,

nested snug in tufts of insulation,

a growing family

of field mice.

Kristina Moriconi

Actually

empty streets boo back
begetting is a national pastime
aloofness is not
what the world is about

give me first-class entertainment
I'll self-sequester in retreat
binge-watch the world thin out
internet the new prince of peace

hold me close in sanitized arms
kiss my soft hygienic face
in my dreams
six feet from yours

I want to stay six feet apart
from the screed poem
I'm not mad at anybody
nor mad at any thing

not the virus   not the economy
there's no need
to scream or shout
actually   I'm very calm

rested   having a lovely
retreat with no talking
actually   I think my brain
is disintegrating   my memory

evaporating   I can't
remember anyone's name
my muscles forget
how to work   time fritters

away faster than warm ice cream
what's left of it   anyway
actually   I want to binge
my life   not the internet

Linda Stryker

Lockdown

time at home is a blank page
an unfilled balloon
waiting for ideas
new breath
to fill its chest.

time passes
slowly and all at once
in drip drop moments like coffee brews
a reminder that some things need time to percolate.

with my body, I wait.

passion stirs
years of thinking, feeling: living
yearning to be built upon.

> *I am not empty*
> *I am not absent of ideas*

back to the grind in my mind, I work.
preparing for the arrival of what's coming.
thinking, feeling, living
not knowing what it might bring.

> *can anyone see beyond the wall of change*
> *not projections, not models,*
> *but really see?*

In my mind, I am free.

Like a plane that's arrived at the gate, locked
COVID 19 is here.
It's after-crisis effects are delayed.

The waves of change aboard
are soon to flood the terminal of human life before it.

Scared? Anxious? Angry?
Me too.
Sleeping? Eating? Staying six feet away?
Me too.

But the truth is: we never know.

I won't let this lockdown lock down my passion
my inspiration, my intellect.

fear
anxiety
sadness
even anger

are kindling for the creation of something beautiful
and new. they feed into the whole picture
are not disregarded
are not hidden

they are seen.
acknowledged.
and used in moderation
for the right purposes
            healing, creative expression
as I wait

prepare
think
and feel

I remember, above all
that hearts
although hurt
are never bound.

So let's create!

Aaluk Edwardson

In and out of Quarantine with Persephone

We forget when Persephone comes back in springtime she's the delicious orchestrator of unruly colors sprouting faster and unholy naked perfume. We roll blossoms or petals in our incredulous hands; we stroll meadows and hear hearts shouting in steady certainty: this won't ever end. Never again will we be deprived or suffer or die. But this is just the beginning of our agonies.

When Persephone returns in spring you may lose sight you missed the cautions when screaming winds send announcements as harsh colliding combustible blooms. How many plays did we see and read together without recognizing we were writing something better than our mouths could shape and stretch and gape at? Urging pulpy pouty lip curves to absurdly re-piece themselves together into unique proportions more in store for us than any precious and previous encounters we swore we couldn't ever forget.

Unsensational and bereft of anxious potential, you missed the end. I'm afraid even now how nothing ever ends, really. How every bare and naked tree quivers and beckons from the ground urging her sound and refound longings; the scorched earth swells and smells of newfound promises in ash. This, I said, reminds me of a campfire; a hearth of hearts you helped me build for you. You fill your mouth with saliva to prepare and there, in moments of dresses at angles and smiles your face didn't remember how to make until the pain ended, you can have the claim of yours again. Yours.

The swelling sweeter swelter of the best touches you've ever encountered as soon as you can endure the ego-ending admissions. She said I almost lost myself in you and I knew from then the ground had become her ally; the expanding sky her friend. It's why airplanes were invented to track sweet hopes into certainty. She got spoiled in all those poem sounds and echoes as the fireworks exploded inside and out; poor Persephone as victim of magnetic molten electricity.

We forget when Persephone comes back in winter she's the orgasmic dictator of fist clutches regaining exhales on our sheets. She says, you don't understand. He isn't anything like you. She leaves and returns and learns only one and one can add to one of us. We see the world as plays and movies because our favorite actress beckons eyes in ivory nightslips; her candy skin as thin and sweet as lilies bending over and reflecting in the tv screen, thick and thicker with soaked up solutions. We can't eat or sleep or shake the stain of headaches until our single needs are solved here. Her lashes cast in nets and get the corners turned of mouths. Of course, of course you always knew this was forever. Our twin delicious predicaments resound in songs or sounds or promises you couldn't help but trust. They're flames; the pomegranate seeds. They're flames.

It's time again. This is just the beginning of exactly what you always knew you'd need. Even if you keep trying to forget this need for inevitable sighing.

Kurt Cole Eldsvig

Isolation Poem with the Destruction of Pompeii

Nydia and her two companions attempt to flee the city after the eruption of Mount Vesuvius. The three become separated, however, and Randolph Rogers captured Nydia as she gropes her way through the burning city. Nydia, the Blind Flower Girl of Pompeii, Art Institute of Chicago

You don't know what to make of
the fact you started dating again eight
months ago and now can't leave
your few rooms except to get a breath
of air and walk briskly around the block,
avoiding all contact. Last August, you
went on a date to the Art Institute
with a man you still talk to, who has
become a confidant about other dates
you go on, and as you're writing this
poem, he texts you a picture of the statue
courtyard in Gallery 161, says that he
hates the idea of them being all alone
in there, especially *Nydia, the Blind
Flower Girl of Pompeii*. She and
the others are all paused mid story,
stone with no one to share their space,
but it's *The Solitude of the Soul*
you're thinking of, figures pulling
free of the marble, one female nude
holding hands with the male figure
to her side while reaching over her
shoulder to another, what sculptor
Lorado Taft said of it: "that however
closely we may be thrown together
by circumstances… we are unknown
to each other." And like Nydia, you
are also paused mid story, groping
your way forward through chaos,
ash and fire somewhere overhead.

Jennifer Finstrom

Ophiostoma ulmi

By a lithe stream awaits a summered elm,
slighter than crucifix, and Christlike thin,
and while the birds sing, birdsong overwhelms,
and weight dryadean inflects the stem.

Beneath the wretched tree I lie and note
the wordlessness of Autumn, and the bruise
the Ambra spreads along her bed, the throat
of rock doves and kaleidoscopic blues.

But then Apollo mars the firmament,
Bacchus blots Paradise with purple swill,
Persephone denies days pearlescent,
so I, denied, droop 'mongst the Daffodil.

So be it. All being winds up curled in bow,
aimless, unanxious, mere material.

Bartholomew Bolander

The Song is Quiet Now

The song is quiet now
Hushed by a lingering promise
A blanket of felt absence, soft as damnation
And just as lonesome as the gates of Eden
Falling shut for the first time, forever

The song is quiet now
A quiet made of locks and cloth
And poison blood and tainted breath
That makes love distance
Catalyzing care into dimming light

The song is quiet now
And the light that is is a shade of itself, shallow
Pooling in the spaces where shadow should sit
Broken by the hollow between leaves
Leaving diamonds scattered in drops for no one

The song is quiet now
Sapped of the will to ring between windows
Down streets and alleys, the byways
Before being washed away with the chorus
That faltered by semitones to stillness

The song is quiet now
But it remains a waiting hum, expectance
Rolling slowly in pavement veins
Under doorstops and window seals
Weaving around the very bottom of things

The song is quiet now
But its echo carries far and fleeting
In the throats of spring finches and the lap of patient waves
That still shudder and shatter and roar
A lion awaiting its audience

The song is quiet now
But remember the tune
Let it fill the hollow with potentiality
With the surety of eternities of dawns and daybreaks
The song, for now, is quiet

Justin Moir

Day 18 of Quarantine: Perspective

Since the world was ravaged by a virus
I have spent much of my time missing things
I am grateful to miss the room with my name
Spelt wrong on the front door
Where I lived with all girls

Comfortable enough to paint on the floor
In oversized men's sweaters and our underwear
Comfortably acknowledging each other in the morning
As we followed our respective routines
Borrowing lipstick and crop tops and everything else

I am grateful to miss the smell of gingerbread coffee
The zest of boxed Franzia White Zinfandel
The lure of Tito's vodka and cranberry juice
While reading Sylvia Plath before
Another basement party with bad music and good people

I am grateful to miss SuperSaver popcorn kernels
Perpetually crushed into threadbare carpet
The living room hammock
The plastic Christmas tree in the corner
Birthday banner on the wall and orange witch who hung
On the ceiling and screamed whenever
We closed a door or set down a dish

I am grateful to miss the blue betta fish named Linda
The resilient, half-dry succulents on the windowsill
The shower with porcelain stained orchid from boxed hair dye
The canvas that never got hung up

I am grateful to miss cutting through campus
To find the quickest way to class
In the big fine brick building with stained glass and bay windows
Where the temperature was never right and
I wrote poetry in the margins of every notebook

I am grateful to miss adrenaline of impassioned class discussions
The chorus of our voices echoing like a revolution
I am grateful to miss a car full of poets on our way
To basements of universities or coffee shops
Where everything became poetry

I am grateful to miss waist-hugs
From elementary schoolers as we lined up for the playground
The routes I could drive with my eyes closed
The view of downtown from the top level
Of the parking garage on P street
$5 movie Tuesdays, and Saturday brunch of greasy hash browns
With gravy and subpar coffee

There are people on the front lines who give me
The privilege to miss these things
Risking themselves to protect and provide
Wearing cloth masks, sleeping in garages,
Driving buses, delivering essentials, caring for the most vulnerable,
Running power, keeping things clean
Generating equipment, delivering mail, serving customers

There are homes that are more war zone than refuge
There are people who must choose
Between self-isolation and starving
There is a world outside my door which is too sick
Too busy, too scared to miss things
Much less write poems about them

Syble Heffernan

100,000

I want to think about school, about
philosophy, poetry, literature, I definitely
do not want to think about a number, especially
not a number like 100,000, not when that
is the low end of an estimate of possible outcome.

I want to think about poetic form, about
functionalism, ontological arguments, the nature of
knowledge and what it means to know a number
like 100,000, what does it take to have knowledge of
a number, to have truth about where our futures lie, to
believe that there is hope around the corner, to
justify making myself try to carry on like
the world is not falling apart,

or is it something more, is there some elusive
condition to knowledge that could help me understand
a number as big as 100,000, or does the key lie
elsewhere? Is there a way to gain knowledge of
the world through effort poured from mind to line that
through the rhymes I might start to find some sort of
understanding of just what a number like 100,000
really
means, what it really costs, what it really

looks like on the landscape of life.

Anthony Mirarcki

unwitting conquests

with all my surplus downtime
I find myself wandering back into
the virtual delights of my youth

and

there's a video game I play
where I face increasingly harder soccer teams
and during the lower levels
I frequently shellack my rivals
11-0,12-2, 14-1
really just givin 'em the business

and because they are pixels
the expression of the opposing players never change
there is no evidence of increased despair
no hunched shoulders, no deep sighs
I score again and again and again

they are the unwitting conquests on my path to glory
they don't know they are just plot points in my
narrative

which leaves me wondering
as I turn off my console
after watching my team of hardened killers
raise the trophy yet again

who am I the cannon fodder for

Michael Hatchett

137

6
Those
Close

139

Moments of Life

seen through screens,
making family connections
from thousands of miles away.

Pictures of smiles and laughter
to show the world that some
bonds can be stretched, but never
broken. Confusion in human error

while the perfect balance is struck
to fit everyone, if not in one room,
then at least in one laptop screen,
one tablet screen, one phone screen.

Moments of life lived through screens
while we black out the apps that remind
us—the world holds chaos beyond our
happy screens—hold these moments close

Anthony Mirarcki

Isolation

My body craves
for your eyes pealing
my clothes away,
or undressing my skin.

I close my eyes and imagine
you are here;
not across continents
flickering through video
frames after frame
and I cannot feel your
breath on my ears.

I can read your eyes,
sunk in moonlight
I can follow your lips
negating my dripping eyes
But I cannot sulk
in the sun of your arms
Dressing up in your odour
sinking in you.

I peel my skin every second,
counting new moons
and killing days
with paper boats
blowing away
Kisses
your way.
my body graves
for your touch

Nida Sahar

grasp-less

the capsized cling to laptops
bottom lines sink

will you fast with me?
eat freedom

grasp-less embodiment
grief release my child

birthed spirit
walk decades undead

here I remain, expanded
midwife ush-plush-usher

in beyond normalcy
forced dimensional bridge

bear down, collected

dilation span
breath

yet here we be
awed ask of creation

Heather Sanderson

Seeds in the Desert

She stands at the windowsill, eyes fixed on the clay jar before her.
I know that look - I've seen it a thousand times.
A smile, suppressed. Bittersweet mix
Of hope and hesitation. Her fingers clasp the handle, tilting the pail.
Droplets of water trickle into the vessel, small and
Cracked at the rim, filled to the brim with parched soil.

The sun has not risen yet when the sound of a
Warning grows louder and louder, approaching our apartment.
I pull her closer and cup her small ears, locking her eyes with mine,
Pulling her face close to my chest. Moments later, the all-too familiar
Roar of a siren. Ambulances are harbingers
Of both hope and sorrow. We have learned to stay low, stay inside
But it's getting harder to breathe. Who knows
What may come. Trying to find refuge behind brick walls
Chipped and eroded by years of neglect and cynicism.

Red lights clash in the darkness. At the table, she eats the
Slice of bread I laid out for her. Before taking a bite,
She offers me a piece. It's ok, honey, I tell her with my eyes.
Her own eyes beckon for answers
Of which I have none to offer. Tendrils of light begin to seep
Through the curtains, giving presence to dust floating in the air.
We watch the sky transform from velvet blue to honey.

The glare of the screen tempts my eyes
But I know the headlines before I even see it; too many, gone,
Numbers that mask faces of people with families.
How can something invisible wreak so much havoc on life?
I can count your age on my fingers and yet
Hurt and pain, illness and dying will be words
Too soon in your vocabulary.
But I don't want to hide the realities of this world from you either.

Can something beautiful still rise from ruins of
Lost dreams, light amidst dust and darkness?
I clasp her hand in mine. Each morning
Brings new mercies. Yes, I will tell her this,
I will show her this. I hope she will never forget.
Seeds grow in deserts, too.

Anna Delamerced

Inundated

Emails like rocks in a mountain slide
crowd my inbox.

Businesses assure me that they
are there for me

that they are taking precautions
to protect me

Some ask for me to please consider their
takeout menu.

Others tell me how to protect
fractured finances.

Many emails relay ways to avoid
COVID19.

Or provide me with gifts of
symptom checkers.

One promises a cure if only
I drink water.

The governor of New York has become
my new best friend

whose reports briefly calm like a cup
of soothing tea.

Meanwhile national numbers like a series of
tsunami waves

smother me each time I
refresh the page.

I await state stats like a nervous newlywed
her husband's touch.

Our doctor daughter, now ill, calls with news: she
has been tested.

My son-in-law also short of breath and coughing.
Both have asthma.

My mind, a whirling sphere, races to my
grandson.
Will he be safe?

Sensing that I may be drowning
my dog climbs up

onto my lap and gazes, steadfast,
into my eyes

each day propelling me outside
into the light.

Johnnie Clemons May

Isolation Poem with Ceres

"Oh you. It's always been you.
Oh my beloved, oh my bedroom wall."
        "Love in the Time of COVID-19," Leah Mensch

This is before you realize quite how serious
everything is, and you make plans to meet a man
for dinner at the Elephant and Castle on West Adams
the day before all of the bars and restaurants close.
Downtown is grey and hollow, someone across the street
sprawled sleeping on a bus stop bench. The statue
of Ceres high atop the Board of Trade reminds you
that you could be walking to meet your date through
the empty streets of the Underworld, souls all blown
away in a cold March wind. You and this man haven't
been communicating well, don't seem to always
understand what the other means, and this won't be
talked about until you're both separately isolated
and you are very drunk. After dinner, he walks to
Union Station to catch the Metra back to the suburbs,
and you wait for your rideshare alone at the side
of the street, don't know when you'll see Navy Pier,
Lakeshore Drive, the streets and shops just blocks
from your apartment again. Spring begins, as cold
as winter, and it isn't until you're writing this poem
that you learn the statue of Ceres you glimpsed
that night has no face, can neither speak nor see.

Jennifer Finstrom

Once Upon A Children's Game

"In a week, an invisible virus turns life upside down"
  -Tacoma News Tribune, March 17, 2020

Not content
with hide-n-seek,
red light/green light,
or kick-the-can, we played
"Invisible Man."
Pretending to be chased
by a fiend who could
not be seen we darted
through yards,
skulked past houses,
and ducked
behind trees,
whipping ourselves
into palpitating frenzies
until, unsure anymore
if the make-believe
was truly fake,
we hid indoors
to shield ourselves
from any ghostly wake.

Barbara Reynolds

Essential

I am writing to remind you that I am essential and you are too.
You are essential to me.
I am essential to the child I built inside my body.
I am essential to the man I share my house with.
I am essential because I feed them.
I am essential because I get the food.

He is Essential.
He is making medicine for you.
He will help you continue to breath.

You are essential.
Without you, he would not need to make medicine.
Without you, doctors would have no patients.

Roads would have no drivers.
The underpaid and brave,
Who are bringers and suppliers of all our essentials and niceties
(which feel even more essential to me now than ever before),
Would have no one to bring to.

We are essential to each other.
It is not too much to ask to remember.

I am essential and you are too..

.

Gemma Webster

Paranoid Hopeless Romantic *(March 10th 2020)*

Panic crawls from my stomach to my chest
and the words die in my throat;
there will not be a funeral for the things never said.

I cannot ask you if you are okay,
cannot be with you to make sure,
cannot tell you that I am terrified
you might not come back to me.

You are not here and now
I know where I want to be,
who I want to be with,
just before the world ends.

Samantha Smith

Reflecting on another time of separation

Two months in the land of bowing,
of dragonflies and rice paddies,
I lay awake, uneasy,
discovering a need, that I did not suspect:
the clasp of masculine hand in hand,
brothers, father, friends and that,
and hugs of friends and mother, sisters,
my flesh demanded others' pressure.

In work each day I boomed good morning,
workmates beamed, half-bowed with nods
but never handshakes, never hugs,
a world of distant courtesy,
of straight back-bending, smiling,
knees locked vertical
like medieval courts of Europe,
still alive in Nagasaki.

There I, so distant and polite,
found to my surprise a need to touch and hold,
embrace and squeeze.
Today I never see
my friends except on screens, my body protests:
the flesh needs more than courtesy.

Shane Leavy

To My Son

The magnolia blooms have arrived
I saw them on my run today
--perhaps my last for a while
no one knows what comes next
in a week or two
the petals will turn brown
fall to the sidewalk
stick to the soles of my shoes
when I run past--*if* I run past

What will I tell you of this time, looking back
the spring when sickness spread like blossoms
from tree to tree, petaled limbs reaching out
longing to touch
What will I tell you of
a world that will soon be yours
of fissures and divisions
the desperate desire for connection

Ask me if I felt afraid and I will say:
the magnolia blooms had arrived

at least there was that
at least there was you

Claire Taylor

When Will He Grow Wings

My father has Alzheimer's -
A visitor in his brain, wandering through rooms
In his memory,
Casually vandalizing the contents
A burglar with no compassion.

We are now almost three weeks into isolation.
We are on day three of near total lockdown.
There are police on the streets of Dublin.
If you are over 70, you must stay at home
You must *Cocoon*.

Like a butterfly, my eldest boy explains, and adds -
When will Grandad grow wings?
But there will be no rebirth, no transformation
No emerging from this for him.
He is not going to spread wings.

I find him in the hall, in his coat and hat.
His arm and voice are raised, both ready for the fight.
He roars at my mother, that he is going for a walk –
God will protect him, he says.

God wants you safe at home, we tell him.
The government want you indoors.
It is the law, we say – and he gives in.
No, he does not understand why.
He watches the news and is afraid,
Then he forgets and wants to go for a walk.
And we are the ones giving him the "no"
And that hard word makes him angry.

My father watches the world through the tv
And the intruder in his mind
Stirs restlessly. He is cocooned like the prey
Caught in a spider's web.

Geraldine Moorkens Byrne

Now That You're Gone

Yes, it's true; I've taken you for granted. I see that
now. It took your leaving to shake me up to how vital
you were to my very existence, my daily routine,

my piece of mind. I never gave any thought to how
you rolled, how you were always within reach, never leaving
my side when I needed you. I was too busy thinking

about me—my needs. Still, you hung around, faithfully
and patiently waiting. Sorry you can't say the same about me.
But it was just that one time. I was weak, and he was so charming

and ultra strong…or so he said! That was just fluff—when shit
got real—he fell apart. Turns out he wasn't wrapped
too tight. And even though he, also, is nowhere to be found,

his words still haunt me, "I'm bigger and longer
lasting than all the rest. I'm the best! I'm the best!"
But not you, Scott, you don't claim to be something

you're not. You get the job done
without bragging about your length
or strength. I want you to know you were more than

just a booty call. Remember that time
you soothed me with your soft touch while wiping my
tears when I cried over loosing what's his name?

See, I don't even remember his name. He never
mattered, Scott. But you do—you matter.
I've never said this before, but

I need you! I want you back. I'm a mess without you!
I miss your practicality, your simple utility. But, most of all,
I miss your availability.

Susan Manchin

In Sickness and In Health

The air is still, dry
We stand before the altar
And rows of empty pews
Stretching back into eternity

Within these walls
I'm trapped, languid
Unborn, floating, fluid
Safe
From the poisonous breath
Of outsiders

When the wind my face
Caresses
With cold fingers
Rubs my skin raw, steals my breath
Pants against my neck
In sinuous whorls
Penetrating
Leaves my hair rumpled
Will I still see the world
Sweat-soaked, gleaming, oily naked
Vast rolling beauty enclosed
Stroked
Smooth beneath human hand
Coated with congealing window?

When the sun my brow
Anoints
My fingers among the grass stems
A vast populace
Steaming
Will I still hear
In the passing clouds
Flick-click
Light-switching behind my eyelids?

But now, what is this joy?
Like a pinprick
A droplet of blood which
Wells
Scarring on the outstretched finger
If I also take his blood
Can I take his hand in mine?

Isabel Hinchliff

Redemption

The pale blue glow has lit up
the nooks and corner of our country
there is a strange closeness
in all the social distancing

we are alone yet together in this fight
the new normal crooks it's head
from the slightly pixelated screens
the cold glow of the pandemic nights

holding our disconnected thoughts in our connected minds
we move like a big ignoramus engine
towards the future:
with anger fear and hope
mixed in equal proportions

the surreal, dystopian ghosts of the future
living in the futuristic shows
have suddenly taken a comfortable pose in the
warm lit corners of our living room

a boisterous unwanted presence;
dispensing justice with the blind eye
equally to the rich and the downtrodden

A new normal
morphed and twisted reality
a bulging curve we are feverishly
trying to flatten yet failing fervently

news pitted with the death of the old and the
suffering
spilling from the rotten edges
of the papers as we stand
here at the edge of humanity

swirling at the epicenter of this pandemic
calling out to our exalted gods in heaven
fervently trying to reason
which one of our seven deadly sins from the past
needs redemption.

Megha Sood

No Time for Spoon River *(To the victims of COVID-19*

"Dear grandparents, it is difficult to let you go like this. You have always told us that without each other you could not live. So, one after the other, just two days apart, you are both in Heaven. We are heartened to think that now you are finally together again and can hug each other once more." (Dante and Angelina's grandchildren from Clusone, Bergamo, Italy)

'Suddenly'
He is gone, in peace.

Quietly, 'suddenly',
She has left us.

'Suddenly'
And nothing else,
For fear of mentioning
The terrible word.

You died alone,
Your soul passing through ventilators,
Forced breath.
No hand to hold yours,
No whispers, no hugs.

Now, you're with the other 156,
Smiling at us from the obituary photos
Filling up the eleven pages
Of the local newspaper.
A few printed lines
The only way to say
We loved you.

Did you comb your hair
Before taking that picture?
Did you wear your favourite lipstick?
Did you use that little square of you
For a new ID or passport,
Or driving licence?
Your coffins line up,

Along the four walls of the church.
I guess you beckon to each other now,
Sharing memories of grandkids' first steps,
Children's graduations,
Fiancées' withered flowers or rings.

Frankincense and myrrh flutter in clouds,
Graze the marble walls,
The stained-glass windows, the cross,
The holy water.
Baptisms, marriages, and funerals
Have the same scent here.

Prayers murmured by the priest
Echo among the forty who departed,
And the few ones
Still kneeling.

At the cemetery,
Only the mourners' eyes speak.
Mouths and noses are covered,
For the dark evil rages in disguise.

Sealed corpses queue,
As if buying
Groceries from heaven's store
Rather than minutes, or the flicker
Of a quick goodbye before burial.

Not far,
There's heat going on, fire,
Non-stop burning,
Smoke—
Like on the *ghats* of Varanasi,
Without the chanting, the ablutions,
Without the river Ganges
Welcoming you in its arms.

They say we are dust
And to dust shall return.

Paola Coronni

161

7
Socio
Politico

163

Sheltering

My weekly Italian tutor asks if I feel safe
about his coming to teach me.
He calls himself a potential viral vector.

Certo, I assure him, knowing he needs
the work. There are two men parked
in my bathroom, carefully installing tile.

Mornings, we bump elbows in greeting,
because we don't share a language
and none of us are the type that prays.

In the late 1800s, it was *mysophobia*,
thought pathological, the constant
washing of one's hands. Now we all

scrub prudently, and hesitate to pet dogs.
There's no such thing as truly safe,
a word which originally meant uninjured;

all of us are injured as, in shops
around the world, people push one another
out of the way over toilet paper and sanitizer,

hoard Chef Boyardee and rice.
In the early 1900s, when TB spread,
men shaved off their long beards, women

wore shortened skirts. When that didn't stop
disease, they blamed immigrants,
like the ones in my apartment, slowly

building a ceramic wall for a shower stall,
not the kind of wall for keeping out,
a soft grey one, for stepping in.

Susana H Case

Crossing the Delaware

I.

George Washington,
where have you been?
Slipped from the ATM
in more innocent times
(three weeks ago),
flimsy token of communicable value,
six minutes of labor
at the current minimum wage,
but currently unemployed,
possible disease vector
quarantined in my black billfold.

II.

A virus almost ended the country before it began. In 1776, smallpox raged through the Continental Army, more fatal to the cause than Redcoat muskets, killing three of every ten.

The public feared inoculation, which was the best defense against the pox, and Congress banned it.

Washington, watching the decimation of his troops, recommended quarantine and inoculation. It had never been done before, inoculation on such a scale, an entire army herded into immunity.

III.

Washington was famous
for his strategic retreats.
To cross the Delaware
was to buy more time,
to wait things out,
to flatten the curve.
To prevail,
sometimes we have to disappear. .

Rob Hardy

A Cadence Inverted

*Come home, stay home, shelter in place_* Hollow
echoes, in the freedom of vacation, sounds forever altered_
Each day a new order, numbers climbing, home-
less populations with nowhere safe to huddle,
11 million undocumented working the front line, fever
or no, for them, little option, nothing different_ For us
the remote world blown up, no more wondering if
work-from-home colleagues can be trusted
with 8-hour days, you worry that there is enough
to fill the hours, you worry about the ones who will end
in ICU_ You call your mother more often, because she lives
alone, and now is not the time to fix that, if ever you really could_   You find
yourself having chest pains because she ventured out, *just
one more aerobics class, just another carton of milk_*

Small businesses hang signs, *temporarily closed, stopping
the spread_* Some will try for the moment, *Carry on,
Carry out, between 4:00 & 9:00 p.m. Delivery on us!*
An early afternoon grocery run, empty shelves, people
on a mission, rice and beans, cans of tuna, coffee, bananas_ Some
wear gloves, masks, no more hand sanitizer_ Neighbors push by
carriages full of toilet paper, the rest of us resort to Depression-
era tricks, recycled newspapers, other things _ You want
to tell them, GI symptoms are the least of our problems_

You watch the video on mute and don't know why
you did it_ The image pans over five pine boxes
laid before the candlelit altar_ No indication of which church,
what town, where on the disease map_ You count more than a hundred
coffins in the end, different shapes and sizes_ Overnight,
deaths mount, footage rolls_ These eternal beds, collect
no dust, tonight the dirge, tomorrow their replacements_

Restaurants turn into community kitchens, meals delivered
to the weary, nurses and doctors working endless shifts, those souls
who can no longer afford their grocery bills_ Each day new
meditations, comfort sought more than found_ calloused, taut_
wood, fingertips, strings_ Humble offerings, virtual gifts,
poplar interlaced with spruce, a cello made in Saronno,   music,
spun from the depths of distance_ And on balconies, you   watch it lift_
multitudes sing, serenading first responders, shouting *buona notte,*
voices here and there in the dark_ You hope
you will be like them, you tell yourself, *if it comes to that.*

Amy Walker

Tsunami

My boyfriend comes home
From another 36 hour shift
Of call after call
Which never seemed to bother him
Unless it was in the middle of the night
But now,
It is the constant donning of
Gowns
and gloves
and respirators
And goggles
That exhausts him.
We will surf for hours today
Him- to wash away
The elderly woman who's house was on fire
But who passed out from the smoke
Before the sprinkler system
Went on to save her life
And when she came too,
In my boyfriend's arms
Shivering and soaked
More at risk of hypothermia
Than smoke inhalation
Said to him with wide eyes
"we made it".
He will surf
for many more hours than I
To wash away
The non existent droplets
That are slowly
and now not so slowly
Infecting his whole department
Six turned to 34 almost overnight
Men who run into burning buildings

Without a fear
Now terrorized by the invisible fire
Burning through bodies
Which they take home unknowingly
To the tow head kids
Jumping for hugs
And to the wife
who leans in for a kiss.
And we both wait
For the tightness in our chest to begin.
He will surf
to wash away work
And I will surf
to do the same
To cleanse my mind and my soul
Of the 400 million masks
We still need to find
To make sure
Our nurses
Our doctors
Our respiratory therapists
Our janitors -wiping the slate clean
Survive the surge
that is descending on us all
Like fog.
We will surf
Despite the sign
that says
"Beaches closed"
Because you can own the land
But the ocean is ours
And those of us who are drowning
On the hard solid ground
Need to find a semblance of sanity
In the sea.

Mali Woods

Just a Nurse

Seventeen and dreaming of being a hero, I became an EMT
It wasn't only the flashing lights and sirens that drew me in
But the trust that people in need placed In a teenager
In a uniform shirt, and the adrenaline that surged
As I exited the rig and stepped onto the scene.

Mostly patients down on their luck,
Drugs and alcohol their chosen vice
A teenager who tried marijuana laced with something sketchy
A season of H1N1 and tropical storm Irene
A 48-hour sleepless shift at the volunteer squad downtown

Two bachelor's degrees and I changed my mind
I became a pediatric nurse in the ICU
A job in which people avoid asking about your day
I was not a hero, but I was important, respected

Twenty-seven and a nurse, a nurse practitioner student
Not dreaming of being a hero, just a nurse
Drawn by the trust that families place in a person in scrubs
And the knowledge and skill to change—maybe save—a life

So many events, in retrospect, that changed everything
COVID-19 pandemic the latest in the news
Thousands dying from a disease some called a hoax
Millions in isolation, unemployment rates climbing

At seventeen, I would catch a train to New York
Drawn by the flashing lights and sirens
Gravitating toward the opportunity to be helpful, be a hero
But the adrenaline dissipates a decade later

I pick up shifts here and there in the ICU
In between virtual graduate classes and projects about
imaginary patients
But the needs are not there yet, mostly empty beds
Perhaps the calm before the storm

There is a relief in cancelled shifts
A chance to avoid exposure, exposing my family
Avoidance of a single mask for multiple days
But there is guilt, too.

Healthcare heroes, chalked on the sidewalk,
Broadcast on the news
The doctors, nurses, respiratory therapists, first responders
They have always been there, thanked, but not remembered;
Their families want them home

I wonder what happened to that seventeen-year-old
The one who wanted to save the world, one patient at a time
Maybe she was never meant to be a hero,
At least not with lights and sirens
Maybe she was always meant to be a nurse

Bridget Noel

Looking for Normal

What the f… is going on?
Where did normal life go?
We cannot just up and go to the
movies when the mood strikes,
cannot sit down at a restaurant,
buy a pair of shoes, watch a soccer
game, or anything else we don't like.

There is nothing to do but watch the news
As the death toll soars beyond reasonable.
From what is far away and bad,
To Washington, then NY, and sad
to lose so many strangers we never knew.

Fears formed from baby on
Always disappear in the daylight ray.
And chances slim, small percentage, it has our name.
But what are these countless stories
of ladies and men in their thirties and forties,
with families and plans and cars and bills to pay
being intubated for a short time before going away?

Chances slim, of course, but now closer to home
the realization seeps, it might not just stay in Rome.
Could be somebody we distantly know,
long lost neighbor of a friend seen
at the edge of a corner a long ago.

Then numbers rise, wide awake, the realization hits:
Holy shit, could get closer than the grocer,
maybe a brother, mother, sister, or worse.
Can't stop these thoughts driving away in perverse

One longs for simpler stress,
The slept on hair that can't un-mess,
The buoyant turd that just won't go down,
Which road to take to get out of town.

We just need to get back to things
little and small that infuriate us all,
back to normal where life is strong
and people bitch all day long.

David Cleveland

N-95

I bought you on the black market,
From a CNA, behind the nurse's station.
I can't blame them for charging me five dollars.
They, along with the doctors, are on the front lines of humanity.
As a social worker, I've never had the humility,
Of wiping a stranger's ass-
Or examining any of their other humors. Directly.

You are asphyxiating. . .Closing the door to my face.
Leaving only the windows of my soul ajar
To offer counsel to my patients.
My job description remains the same. I'm a hustler of jargon,
Perseus' reflective shield, a soother of patient's —Psyches—
 How I don't want them in union with God too soon.

Yesterday administration decreed
That I'm not to enter the infected's rooms.
Who is the leper? The patient or me?
White coat syndrome might be more real now—for them.
COVID-19's proteins unpin order.
The helix of their pernicious DNA unthreads social
Fabrics that ostensibly protect me from the virus.

The governor says there is not enough of you,
For us first responders. But to whom should I respond?
To common civility? Upon which I have honed my tongue
For the past ten years in social-work school.
To the fear-mongering media? Which is not allowed in here.
To press the flesh-- To shake hands—
With a death that pends for all—But when?

When I am at work? In this masquerade from nine to five?
When I clock out, on a pleasant spring day?
When I walk outside all move six feet over-Save the pigeons.
Walking, bobbing their heads. Strutting, mocking me.
As if they remember those quacks Of the 17th century
Wearing their manner on their faces Loading them with incense
That stinks like the weed of the hobos I pass.

I hide my I.D. which allowed me to *Danse Macabre*
Without threats of a fine for another day.
I amble past a liquor store, another "essential" business.
But, let's be charitable, they are giving free rounds
To us healthcare personnel dealing with this new *Vita Nova*.
I'll still pay the mortgage for my house on time.
A dead pledge to the fate I tempt daily.

The president wants America open by Easter.
Maybe he can fill Tetzel's coffers singlehandedly for the living,
but does he care about the dead in the hospital morgues?
I want to give him the benefit of the doubt.
I tear you off my face and throw you in the wash—
I'll don Luther's Ninety-Five Thesis again tomorrow
When I return to work at the nursing home.

Peter Prizel

(Also published in the Northern New England Review)

Dog Walking in the Global Pandemic

The man in the black mask veers to one side
and almost shudders when we pass.
He wants only to survive this dog walking stuff
and return home where his wife is booting
up a Zoom meeting, and will ask, how'd it go?
I shiver too, stepping the requisite feet away,
into the strange *pas de deux* we perform
nowadays, allowing him with his elderly Scottie
some degree of assurance that we
are in the same humanhood
as all those who have embraced the national
pastimes of Purell hoarding, counter wiping,
Lady MacBethy hand washing, all of us
waxed more scrupulous than the DEA.
Surely we both revolve the tissue roll
as gently as a lock we have forgotten
the combination to, a ritual which oddly
makes us feel sane. Each time we masked
strangers pass can be accounted an accomplishment
of sanity, as if the global pandemic has given all
those boring years of wait and see,
of trying and failing a focus, so simple in its splendor,
so much like the stunted movement of the Neanderthals,
or the Plains Indians, or priapic pioneers, live or die,
motherfuckers, live or die. Even our mortgages
have been suspended. We could be
astride horses, or tracking deer for lunch, avoiding
rattlesnakes and mountain lions and grizzlies.
Despite everything, I want to shake his hand.
Finally everyone is lonely and in danger.

Every tribe is lonely and in danger and for good reason,
not because we aren't rich enough,
or hot enough, or young enough
but because a gazillion common
invisible enemies pursue us indiscriminately,
and thus we all are hurrying back
to our homes, like caves once
filled with Gregorian chant,
but now where someone we may
have gotten tired of lately, looks up,
and says, fascinatingly, how'd it go?

Dorie LaRue

Making Anagrams Great Again

I'm *a spiny clone* of *Nancy Pelosi*,
    shredding the speech of *Donald Trump*,
        praying we'll *dump* our *tan Lord*.

He condemns kneelers while perched
    on his star-spangled *bone spurs*,
        a nerveless *borne puss*.

He chooses a *Supreme Court* nominee,
  who'll crawl *up Roe's rectum*.

But when he targets *Obama's Biden*,
    an idea bombs, like the wall and his promise
        Mexico will pay for it,
        a wormy foil, explicit in lies,

resulting in the House's duty to *impeach Trump*,
  refusing to *permit a chump* to obstruct.

I notice his *loyal cronies*, delivering *royal con lies*,
        serving the Chief *oral so nicely*.

There's *Mayor Rudy Giuliani*, a warrior wading
        in Russian dirt, just a *guy amid urinary oil*,
            hunting the rumored blackmail tape.

I ignore the preacher and his *hymnal gas ride*,
        Lindsey Graham, whom *I grandly shame*.

I predict the snake's *hiss, fragmented acid*,
        hanging from his fangs, puncturing twins,
            a *Friday Night Massacre*.

He confesses, *it's our itch, honestly,*
to reign elite over every *shithole country.*

But I panic, seeing the *Coronavirus Task Force,*
  Pence leading the *carnivorous croak fest.*
    In *a furor, I overstock cans.* I either await this
stark vaccine of ours *or* hoard soap and Clorox.

Still, I sleep in peace, wrapped in the *First Amendment,*
  knowing Freedom of Speech is the *finest damn term.*

I tell my critics *don't call me unpatriotic,*
  no undiplomatic clatter shall
    prevent my *political rant document.*

They mistake *proper wit* for a *power trip.*

I just *want filters* for *Flint's water.*

I cringe at hopes of opening for business on *Easter Sunday,*
  the *sedentary USA* packing the pews.

Listening to our *wartime president,* I fear the pandemic *repeats midwinter.*

Nancy Santos

"This is a War"

Is it really, Mr. President?
If so, who is the enemy? Whom
should we kill? A faceless
virus? Something alive inside
our human bodies?

The enemy cannot be
us, the human hosts, the victims
in hospitals, senior centers,
hospices, or at home, separated
from what is familiar, isolated
from those we love, scared
of the unknown—this new place
where we are no longer in control
of our lives, of nature, or of others.

We cut trees to build
us comfort and luxury.
We own, kill, and eat
animals, whereas equal
opportunity viruses
like the Corona
invade us humans and
crown themselves kings

Do we declare war on hurricanes,
tornadoes, floods, and fires?
If this is a war, Mr. President,
we started it many years before now.
It is a war against nature, our mother,
and we have everything to lose.

Let's stop calling it war and stop
thinking of winners and losers,
of heroes and villains, of conquerors
and conquered. We are all connected
as branches of the same tree, feeding
from the same roots, breathing
the same air, warmed by the same sun.

This is not a war, Mr. President,
but the time for us, humans, to work together
and to realize for once that our actions
impact more than ourselves. Our actions
can hurt others, including the Earth, our home,
the Earth that we don't own, the Earth which,
if we don't care enough to protect, won't
protect us from each other.

Mari-Carmen Marin

Go

Come here now, I want to speak to you
You with your millions of tears and swollen tongues
We are tired of your spread, your dread,
your indiscriminate fear,
your march down our throats
Go!

Why can't you be accommodating,
quiet and small, like your brethren in our guts?
Your headaches are scaring the children
Your fevers are infecting the Yayas and Papaws
Your taking of breath is singularly and spectacularly despised
Leave!

Run away with yourself and hide in dung heaps
Stew alone in cesspools and sludge ponds where you belong
Play with bats and rats for all we care
And take your goddamn lust for panic with you,
you selfish spore
Die!

For Chrissakes just leave us in peace,
so we can get back to the business of
warring our enemies, killing the climate,
unforgiving trespasses and
being sick of each other
Please?

Hugh Findlay

We Didn't Think It Would Be Us Next

On the news, we watched other cities go silent
whole streets left for the ghosts, tarmac graves
millions hiding inside, endless scrolling trying
to fill the hours with something other than dread.

In Italy we saw videos of strangers singing to each other
from balconies like mournful birds, weaving hope
and solidarity through the air with their voices
reaching through the dark in the hope of an answer.

We didn't think it would be us next,
the illusion of safety too strong until it shattered
and we were the ones fighting this invisible war
a quiet war of distance and lonely deaths in
hospital wards splitting at the seams.

In supermarkets there are gaping chasms where the flour
and eggs once were, a nurse sleep-walking through
bare aisles as the day's dead flash in the dark spaces
behind her eyes each time she blinks.

On an empty tube a teacher wears her mask like a flag
not for herself, but for the children she'll teach in the day
for her diabetic mother she'll come home to that night.

We didn't think it would be us next,
but now it is and we're learning new ways to live
learning how to fight by not fighting at all
learning how to rise each time we fall.

Annmarie McQueen

United States of Virus

America, Eliot was right;
April is the cruelest month, breeding
Greed out of a viral wasteland, mixing
Life and death inside screaming hospitals, stirring
Nurses and doctors into sweaty mask zombies
Who abandoned their families
To love other people's loved ones
To make stranger-saving god decisions
In the suicide periphery of daynight
While pleading to fascists and sycophants
for machines that can breathe
Life into the terrified,
And some die alone and become
neatly arranged ice packages,
Inside white curbside dumpsters
As America's president sucks
the one percent in bailout brothels
As those who don't believe in science
make science decisions
As those who are 'pro-life' kill people
via church gatherings
and stock up on guns
for the supermarket apocalypse

And as millions become unemployed
desperate, and destitute
And as new life is brought into the world,
Spring will have wrought
Democracy
to its
grave.

Maxine Nodel

Sticky Squeeze

Citizenship years ago
as if I were not real before
chill conversation with a figure of authority
with the authority to determine
my ability to integrate to belong to phrase
no big deal
I *passed* easy peasy privileged
knowing nothing

In 2020 citizenship can no longer be formalized
without the good old handshake
the sticky squeeze of strange fingers
from cold and limpid to
crushing contest
and everything in between

The little buffet of dead
skin cells and bacteria
prohibited to combat the virus

So how do people get their long-awaited citizenship?
Replace the handshake with a more hygienic
greeting?
Wear latex gloves?
Trust the procedure and waive the handshake?
Put humans above symbols?
None of the above just put people on standby?

Have a guess...

Cindy Lynn Brown

187

8
This
Spring

189

The World Has Changed, But There is Hope

The World Has Changed. Our language is now one peppered with key phrases such as "stay at home" "flatten the curve" "self-isolate" and "social distancing" - all now common parlance, along within "coronavirus" and "covid-19". Thousands have died, hundreds of thousands infected, and millions of people - families, friends, and colleagues, touched by tragedy.
The world has changed.

The World Has Changed. Media channels cannot go by for a single moment in time without mention of one of these phrases. Most live TV programmes are cancelled or now in webcam conference rooms, social gatherings of more than two are banned, and anger wells in twitter feeds and Facebook threads. The world has changed
.
But There is Hope - those same twitter feeds and Facebook threads also produce communication, contact, humour, entertainment, and information - important information which keeps us together (while apart) and safe. There is hope.

There is Hope. There are universal events, such as Clap for our NHS, and people singing together from their individual balconies; there is good will, shows of solidarity, the best of humanity is overwhelming the worst; not to mention the plethora of humorous memes and gifs, and giant gatherings of social virtual crowds - each person separate and safe. There is hope.

The world has changed, but there is hope.

Trevor Maynard

In These Times We Keep

In these times that we keep
Words feel so cheap
They could drown you to sleep
But if the costs were more steep
Like if rhymes were a dollar
More vowels we would swallow
Who's howls do we follow
In these times that we seek
Words cut so deep
Like masks for the sheep
Or graves for the weak
Our prayers seem so hollow
Darkened by sorrow
What path shall we follow
In these times that we weep

Michael Belmore

Speak To Me Of New

I sit on the green
of the carpet,
lamplight my shine,

Wildflowers rooted
in the wallpaper,
clouds painted
eggshell white

Hanging
in a small closet,
spring in need of spring

There was a bird
in the grocery this week,
there are dolphins
swimming the canals
of Venice

I am reminded daily
that I am bullets
and petals

Catherine Felty

Never-ending Sun

Run away with me,
To a place where the things we worry about don't matter,
Where the sun melts into the sky,
And the birds sing so beautifully we forget the sun never sets.
Stay here with me in the paradise of our own making,
Dancing and play in the sunflower field,
And we can laugh without worrying about the wrinkles around our eyes,
Blinded by the magnificent blooms.
The sun never sets,
So we never have to worry about the night and her stars,
Or wonder if the moon misses the sky,
Wonder is the stars truly do light up the sky,
Where are you stars…
Did the moon take you…?
She can't. The sun never sets,
Eclipses anything, everything else,
Here we are, trapped in the paradises of a never-ending sun,
Dancing and spinning and laughing until we cry,
Never noticing the stars were hidden behind our eyes this whole time.

Kristen Corbisiero

Pandemic (5) – Possibilities

When the pandemic paralyzed our world
the protracted period of enforced inactivity
allowed us all ample time to imagine our lives
post-apocalypse

Upon sincere reflection
we collectively realized our fervent wish
and ultimate goal
was for nothing to ever be
as it once was

MK Punky

Hope

It's a strange time of our existence, precariously balanced
like an erratic … my little brother is unwell, so is one of my

best friends counting his lonely instants in the jaded eyes
of a caring nurse or the sweet cacophony of NYC, ICU;

discordant and yet filled with a promise of a better
tomorrow; it's time to ponder about the lofty; and of the

eternity's cold and lonely certitude. Last night the moon
did not refuse to lend its lanky rays to the tulips still to

bloom for spring time festivity; and the birds still did dive
to pick the kernels from my open hand.

M Zaman

Spring 2020

Outside my window, cold pale morning sun
thaws stubborn straggles of snow, strikes
starlings tentative on dark branches of bare maples-
silhouettes etched against a grey and cloud-piled sky.

A single runner jogs along deserted streets.
Silent roads these days, not business as usual.
We hear of mayhem in the markets, sickness in the city.
Covid 19. Three to date. Cooped up. In quarantine.

Later on, we rise later than usual, drink mugs
of coffee and read the latest numbers: twenty-eight
confirmed and more to come. Like flocks of blackbirds
wheeling down the wind. A murmuration of sorrows.

In this time of Covid carnage, life transformed
by lockdowns, when each day more dreams are killed
and the planet's closed to commerce, this is the time
for my own inventory, a message for correction.

Time to search through old boxes in my brain,
keep what's meaningful and worthy, toss
what is not. Hold closer, loved ones I want to talk to,
let go those I don't. Note the excess, weed out the rest.

Enough of that, It's April now. The feeble sun
grows stronger, timid snowdrops dare to bloom,
starlings will make again their messy nests
In stolen clefts.

Nan Williamson

A Prayer for the Sequestered

May your home become a hermitage
of quiet contemplation
As though you were out in the desert
seeking the light in solitude
Or may it become a hothouse
of tomatoes and ideas
Unaccustomed to such attention
May your four walls enclose you
With safety and then vanish
As you look out onto the trees
Filled with birds that sing
And flaunt their freedom
May you savor the abundance
Of pantries filled with soups
And dried pasta awaiting sauces
May you remember the words
To the songs you danced to
And find your feet dancing again
May you remember your mom
Or maybe your dad confined
To a bed or wheelchair
Who you thought were
Bounded like Hamlet
In a nutshell but counted
Themselves kings and queens
Of infinite space

Carol Flake Chapman

the morrow

time dissolving into itself
a shapeless continuum
of hours and days
of sadness and isolation
vulnerable flesh concealed
by masked fear
only buildings
concrete and steel
stand in quiet defiance
emptied streets lie silent
under the pounding hooves
of the Pale Horse
just as light turns
into cover of darkness
the sun will rise
bestowing a new day
illuminating hearts and souls
for we are
no ancient civilization
to lie in ruin
for future generations
we will discover
today is not our last tomorrow.

Abby DeSantis

After

After
could we rise from our sickbed
to a world cured of its viruses,

the poisons
that have seeped and tunneled
into its sentient tissues

to madden its brain,
calcify its heart,
murder it

in the sleep of its unreason,

money lust
driving it to suicide
before market bulls,

hate
erupting into blame,
numbing it to cruelty,

denial
of plain truth, lulling it
to the siren song of idiocy,

distraction
turning it in all directions
from the clarity of need?

What vaccine
could dissolve the walls
that make us pathogens

against the larger body?

After
could we wake to find
it's finally immune?

Cary Barney

This Spring

The fresh, sweet smell of bridal wreath
Sweeps into the clear, sun-drenched air
Thrush, starling, and finch chatter
Blackbirds clunk down, swallows soar high
Though I've not seen a robin this spring

We have four cats
A Bengal-striped Georgie
A, grey and white fluffy, pantalooned Lily
The traditional black and white Boston
And a tabby, peach patchwork that is Willow
They pad the grass circle; the paving crazed and cracked
Leap to the wooden bridge by the pagoda
Chase dragonflies across the skein
Stretched between the stepping-stones of the murky pond
Though I've not seen any frogs this spring

An owl hoots, wood pigeons coo
a bumblebee bounces on a barely perceptible updraft
There are cars still passing across the railway line
Clapping their hard rubber tyres on cool steel rails
Distantly a jack hammer jacks, and above
A single 'plane, seeming glass in the reflecting light
Scratches the pristine blue
I've watched, and read the news, I love my family
Though I've not seen my kith and kin this spring

The inevitability of the year marches on
April proclaiming Easter Sunday for some
May, our China wedding anniversary
June, the birth of our first grandchild
I am confident a robin will show
Frogs will once more become the playthings of our cats
My parents and my grandchildren will play hide and seek again

I've walked outside my garden to the street
To the canal, the park, the supermarket
Thankfully I've not seen the usual bustle
I am grateful for the quiet, but crave cacophony
Statistically our chances of survival are overwhelming
But one death is a ripple that affects us all

This spring
There are many things we have not seen
Many things we hope to never see again

Trevor Maynard

And's & But's of Quarantine

This is not new. Quite the opposite.
But how lucky we are, now, to be safe within our home,
Barricaded against an invisible tide.

How lucky we are to have an endless stream of entertainment
And a fully stocked refrigerator.
How lucky we are to virtually visit our families, our friends,
To attend meetings and classes.
But it does not feel lucky.

How lucky I am to have a job—
Reduced hours, but income nonetheless.
How lucky I am to be a nurse, to be skillful, be useful.
But I do not feel lucky.

How grateful I am to have a partner,
A family to live in isolation alongside.
How grateful I am to have friends who call, text,
Attend virtual happy hours.
But I still feel lonely.

How relieved I am that the epicenter is not in my city.
How relieved I am that my family, friends, neighbors are well.
But I still feel anxious.

How confident I am that this is only temporary.
How confident I am that we—
As a country, as a humanity—will learn from this.
But at what cost?

How scared I am that I will become sick.
How scared I am that my family will fall ill.
And then what?

How I grieve for those healthcare workers
Who decide how to allocate resources.
How I grieve for those that are dying alone without a hand to hold.
And what about their families?

How angry am I that there are those that
Do not recognize the gravity of our reality.
How angry am I that there are too few masks,
Unreliable information, and weak leadership.
And yet we remain hopeful.

How lucky we are to be resilient—
As communities, a country, a humanity.
How lucky we are to be compassionate, driven, and innovative.
And this too shall pass.

Bridget Noel

3/11/20

first sign of color in
my garden
cherry blossom official
oh, it's a dream
heart filled
with gratitude
is it time to
remember the joy and
not feel as heavy
one thing that
cheered me up
was a friend saying
there are some
hard realities
happening right now
let's please not
pretend they
aren't happening
and not be
crushed by
them either
kind and
compassionate
souls are
needed now more
than ever
have you
met us yet
I feel so
completely blessed
to be one of
the lucky ones
tag yourself and
let me know what
you are

Wendy Grossman

Spring Postponed

A haiku sequence

streamed lives -
on a chestnut twig's shadow
blooming buds

delayed March
the birdless balconies
of bare branches

movie date
in the tenement stairway
popcorn scent

falling plum blossom
new cases of covid
each day

silent streets
past years' murmur from a
photo album page

last chess game
instead of a sickle
he carries a crown

end of pandemic
a hawthorn wreath bearing
its first fruits

Judit Katalin Hollos

9
Nature

209

Those Eyes of Mine

As I felt the sun on my shoulder
Burn through the straps there
I shifted my pack to the other side
And took a look to the mountain
I blinked at first
Those eyes of mine
Wanting
Needing
When I opened them I saw the green
Grown thick from the spring rains
And knew I could trust it
Absolute
For the sun will shine and the rain will fall
And the seeds push out of the soil
I know because these things have no opinion of me
If I live or die
And because they don't I can take and take
Mold the sights into putty
And fill the holes punched out of my body
And know they will hold
Know they will be there even if I'm not

Brandon S C Brewer

Shelter In Place

Along our drive the dogwood blossoms lift
Their pale cross faces to a soft gray sky
Drawn damp beyond an oak. A few drops sift
Through its red-green-gold leaves. Two cardinals fly,
Then perch among the blooms. Under the eaves
A house wren on his nest calls for a wife.
After each finch, each red-breast robin leaves,
These songbirds still accompany my life.
I need an aviary for my heart:
Perfect blue eggs well-sheltered in a nest,
Birds of bright plumage, notes that pierce the breast.
Under my breastbone feathered wingbeats start.
Uplift my spirit, variegated birds,
Past the great grief which transcends human words.

Sara Cupp Smith

The Frozen Spring

Chills still in the spring air
Three snows buried the dirt
I blew on the windowpane
Breath fogging the glass
I drew a cat in the misted window
Streetlights came on
My cat had amber eyes
Two mischievous faces
Face to face in silence

Cigeng Zhang

Settlement

As dust settles
ever thicker
on the hoods of cars
and the roofs of silent houses
the air shivers
with what's left of the birds
as if they've just found their voice
and with it, a foothold
on a sky no one thought
could be blue again.

The roads we used to take
are strewn with leaves
and strays napping belly-up
on the afternoons
moving only when they need to
shoo a fly or scratch
their backs against the pavement
because the world hasn't stopped
for any of them.
Tonight, they will hunt
like they always have
while the flowers retire
to bloom again in daylight.

Anne Carly Abad

A Fallout unspoken

The air about us in
The coming of Spring
Feels a little more still now.
A bit more static,
Almost solid.

Gray, it hangs low, this
Concrete sky.
Impenetrable,
It casts silence over
The city that can't seem to wake.

Sullen city
Doesn't know where to turn.
Living herein,
Standing afar, it's
Whispers lie dormant.

And the pall that holds us
We thought would arrive with
Howling boom and argent glow
Carries instead
A fallout unspoken.

John Pietaro

'tween times

'tween times
the water's surface
grew rich in spawn
marchin' on thru
april soon; where will we be then?

a hiatus in factory smoke
no acid rain, or smog
a beautiful sunny day on which
bodies wait to be buried
'tween times; waiting for
the tadpoles to lose their tails
community to build in the community

marchin' thru
may, june – frogs have grown
left the pond, many will die
waiting for the surge
bodies piled high
'tween times

Brian M Falconer

Vernal Equinox Lockdown

The sun shone down on empty streets.
The roads breathed, free of traffic.

As if leaves were notes, the wind
had a different song for different trees.

Fox tails swayed in unison. A soloist,
the morning dove kept asking *Who?*

backed by the mocking birds' mimicry.
With invisible thread, flitting wings

in the bloom-scented air seemed
to connect equally all living things

except for the sheltered in shrinking
rooms locked in behind shut doors.

June Ellen Glaser

Anthropocene Sin

Let my worry settle like a bird settling on the tender
twig on the tall cotton-silk tree in the yonder nooks

of my childhood's memory; or with the music emanating
from my mother's golden bangles; I am tired of this inane

pandemonium; of this vacuity of daily vagaries;
"Life is nothing but a walking shadow" - is it not?

But how do I settle my torpid mind; life's shelves are
empty; so are the shelves of my neighborhood store…

They are tiny bugs, they have come; and the Sapiens of
this Earth cringe in deathly fear; aren't we supposed to be

wise and burning with an *'affirming flame'*? Yes, the humanity
shall survive, and this earth still be teeming with billions

of bipeds going their own way; eating, drinking, and being merry
unbeknownst of the fact that WE, the wise ones, the masters of

this Holocene epoch, systematically killed the mastodons and
ravaged every non-human habitat in an orgy of

an Anthropocene Sin.

*"Wrathfully and violently earth comes out of earth;
and gracefully and majestically earth walks over earth.
Earth from earth builds palaces and erects towers and temples,
and earth weaves on earth, legends, doctrines, and laws.*

*Then earth becomes tired of the deeds of the earth and
wreathes from its halo, dreams and fantasies.*

*And earth's eyes are then beguiled by earth's slumber
to enduring rest. And earth calls unto earth:*

*I am the womb and the sepulcher, and I shall
remain a womb and a sepulcher until the plants
exit no more and the sun turn into ashes". (*Kahlil Gibran)*

Today, on this first day of vernal sunshine when the hyacinths
and the primrose are about to burst out of the cold and cruel

winter spell, just as the tiniest bit of a living RNA, coronate
with a corona of pretty spikes of mortal kiss, trying to make

its own living a little cozier, WE, the Sapiens are still hell-bent
on burning the very abode of all that breath and birth their offspring;

this verdant ball; this cerulean ocean, and the verdure of undulating
paddy fields; you and I, and these puny little strands of viral RNA…

It's the only ship, it's the only abode, a journey of togetherness into
death's end.

M Zaman

(*"Out of Earth", from "Thoughts and Meditations" by Kahlil Gibran)

Tiny Bay

*"The rooster who took credit for the sunrise is outraged to be blamed for
the sunset," David Frum.*

I haven't yet snagged a glimpse of him.
but in my imagination he swaggers about
boorish and bloated. His wattle flapping
like an oversized red tie against his inflated chest.
A ruby crown, an obnoxious cap cockily set
on his puny head. Ample feathers of rusty hue,
freakish and perverse.

Tiny Bay balms us into passivity.
Cumulus clouds, mirror images of sea turtles
that slyly poke their heads above water
or herons that dry themselves on rocks
by the shore. A juxtaposition to a world
thrumming in crisis and instability.
Yet, the unseen rooster cock-a-doodle-dos
us to fret over what we would prefer
to blot out with local rum and a tranquil, turquoise sea.

At night, under flimsy mosquito netting
I attempt to thwart the rooster's caws with ear plugs
and a fan that whirs white noise. But he pierces
my winsome dreams with his caustic crows. Squawking
wake up calls hours before sunrise.

My morning swim, a daily meditation.
Noiseless fish dart about. No tides' pull
or boats' wake drag me off course.
My breath and strokes, calm, rhythmic.
Their magnified decibels, obscure the rooster's crow.
Quickly, I raise my head to gauge my surroundings
but his emphatic yawps pervade my placidity.

The subtle sigh of waves, murmur of palm fronds,
and trilling island thrush are useless
in obliterating his cries. His spasmodic clucks
rouse me to consciousness, startle me
from impending stupor. This is not the time
for abstraction. The wretched,
raving rooster won't permit it.

Laurie Rosen

An Echo Through Pelagic

When dusk descends
on the world we knew
and the vapid walls of home
grip our days
the gaze turns inward
and the winter of the soul
gathers purpose
and wool

Strange
troubling
sobering
we say
try to wrap words
around a bending shape
clawing for meaning
combing for seeds

The wheel slows
flickers
stops
the one we've watched for years
blindly
and still the drumming deepens
an echo through pelagic
some confess they see a stain
lifting from the fabric

Amidst the quiet moments
that we count and sculpt and cradle
the soft winds
of tomorrow
are writing a new fable:

Despair is an open window
they whisper through the fog
extraordinary fruit
is ripening
before you

Samantha Stone

All Back In Place

Trees, spring flowers…all blossoming buds
Meanwhile I'm still wearing the same old duds.

I go to the store and find limited goods,
No toilet paper, no Lysol; I'll just head to the
woods?

As eagles fly high, the prices soar;
How the hell will we manage, and feed the poor?

Rent is behind, due to this 'Flu',
They're closing the door of businesses too!

Stay home, don't be a hoarder;
All I can think of is food I can't order!

Time to clean …
Time to bake …
I wonder if this is all a 'fake'?

Walk your dogs, more time with the kids;
Can we adjust; while the stocks hit the skids!

Social media, keeps us connected
Work from home; don't get infected!

Grandmas and Grandpas, no visitors can see
I am grateful for healthcare workers; give them
PPE!

Blindsided by covid, but not lost in faith;
Mother Nature will put it all back in place.
.

Susan Fleming

Maybe We Will All Become Butterflies: A Vision

Here we are in our cocoons spaced six feet apart
Suspended from branches in our own yards
Not knowing what to do here alone in the dark

We were just hungry worms munching our way
Through bountiful banquets of green leaves
When the order came to suspend everything

We were fat and full of ourselves as we ceased
Our restless urge to eat everything in sight
And went silent and quiet in this new fad diet

Some of us began singing inside our bindings
But we soon began to lose our wide mouths
And everything we had ever been or wanted

We were turning to mush before we knew it
But somewhere inside us were imaginal cells
That held the deep secret of transformation

These separate isolated cells began to talk
To each other and to come together in a new way
Creating a totally new being that grew wings

And lo and behold we outgrew those bindings
And we emerged whole into the light with
The desire to fly and seek the sweetest nectar

On this surging and seething earth that awaited us
In this new guise that did not dig or trample or build
But floated free for a time from blossom to blossom

We had to lose ourselves before we gained this
Knowledge that all along we were awaiting
The chance to grace the earth with our beauty

Carol Flake Chapman

227

Alphabetical index of first lines

229

"I will talk as a friend."	73
1. Covid-19, social distancing	109
A spreader used to be a lorry	
that made roads safe in winter	78
After	199
After the pandemic	32
Along our drive the dogwood blossoms lift	211
America, Eliot was right	185
And the news comes on	65
As dust settles	213
As I felt the sun on my shoulder	210
at the empty streets and the hallowed lanes	49
before	16
Before our fears hovered on every face	62
broadway is dark	14
By a lithe stream awaits a summered elm	130
Chills still in the spring air	212
Citizenship years ago	196
Come here now, I want to speak to you	185
Come home, stay home, shelter in place	167
Covid	92
Covid-19	25
Dark circles under my mother's eyes	57
Days go by	115
Don't sweat the big stuff	50
Don't want to get up	94
Emails like rocks in a mountain slide	145
empty street boo back	123
first sign of color	205
George Washington	164
Got the coronarvirus	91

Here we are in our cocoons spaced six feet apart	224
How is it that something intangible can bind us	68
How strange to awake to the singing robins	39
I am the elder	36
I am writing to remind you I am essential	149
I bought you on the black market	176
I check the news (a click of automation)	45
I couldn't breathe right	86
I fish the world out of my pocket	97
I got out of bed today	51
I had a glimpse, for a split second	75
I have killed my millions	84
I haven't yet snagged a glimpse of him	219
I know the many forms of guilt well	102
I must go down to the shops again	90
I sit on the green	192
I wake in purgatory, where I hear	76
I want to think about school	135
I've watched you walking, as you wished	72
If I washed my hands	24
I'm a spiny clone of Nancy Pelosi	179
In the intersection of three circles, I live	13
In the private hive of a public restroom	101
In these times that we keep	191
Inside days are a blur	47
Invisibility I say when my son asks	46
Is it really, Mr. President?	181
It feels	77
It takes time to feel comfortable in a war zone	70
It's a strange time of our existence	195

It's one am before I decide	*19*
Last night I dreamed	*117*
Let my worry settle like a bird settling on the tender	*217*
Man in a blue face mask	*69*
March 18: New Mexico closes restaurants and bars	*55*
May your home become a hermitage	*197*
Mundanity curves over the cloud	*29*
My bedroom	*40*
My body craves	*141*
My boyfriend comes home	*169*
My cat	*98*
My father has Alzheimer's	*153*
My friends' texts pop up like crocuses	*38*
My kids won't load the dishwasher	*99*
My pet bat has the Corona virus,	
but she's asymptomatic	*103*
My weekly Italian tutor asks if I feel safe	*164*
Native or immigrant, your barbed wire	*83*
No matter how late I wake up I still make breakfast	*53*
Not content	*148*
Not gonna follow the Curve //////////	*107*
Old office phone, the incessant bell,	*64*
On the news, we watched other cities go silent	*184*
Outside my window, cold pale morning sun	*196*
Panic crawls from my stomach to my chest	*150*
People are raining down dead in New York	*100*
Routine! Without it we'd be lost, as well we might	*31*
Run away with me	*193*
seen through screens,	*140*
Self-Monitor and Practice	*67*
Seventeen and dreaming of being a hero	*171*
She stands at the windowsill, eyes fixed	*143*
Since the world was ravaged by a virus	*133*

Slowing down we stroll don't run	27
speak to me	17
streamed lives	206
'Suddenly'	159
Temporary measures are in place	105
The air about us in	214
The air is still, dry	155
The Bermuda grass falls out	52
The box	48
The cellist sits down in her wicker chair	115
The day is chilly and grey and eerie	12
The far-off war is here now	28
The fresh, sweet smell of bridal wreath	201
The magnolia blooms have arrived	152
The man in the black mask veers to one side	177
The morning light is odd, the sky	43
The pale blue glow has lit up	157
The ravine walls of opposite blocks	37
The song is quiet now	131
The sun shone down on the empty streets	216
The World Has Changed. Our language is now one	190
This is before you realize quite how serious	147
This is not new. Quite the opposite	203
time at home is a blank page	125
time dissolving into itself	197
Tonight, lock yourself down	110
Tree, spring flowers	223
'tween times	215
Two months in the land of bowing	151
two steel poles	93
Veiled beneath layers of mesh	20
walls of glass	58

We forget when Persephone
                       comes back in springtime   127

We had to pack up most of our home   41

We have all become our dogs it seems   96

We have broken down our morning to the essentials   15

We ripped out the lilac bush.   95

We search for release in unimportant ways   21

we stop asking where   79

We went walking   23

we were already distant   18

What I think of   80

What if the nurse weighs you   71

What the f... is going on?   173

When dusk descends   221

When the factories stop   108

When the pandemic paralyzed our world   194

Who do you love? (Assignment #8)   117

with all my surplus downtime   136

Yes, it's true, I've taken you for granted   154

Yes, you might say, I'm a little obsessed   63

You don't know what to make of   129

You said: Let's meet in New York at 3 in the morning   114

235

BIOGRAPHIES

237

Anne Carly Abad   *Pandemic (we are many) / Settlement*

Anne received the Poet of the Year Award in the 2017 Nick Joaquin Literary Awards and has been nominated for the Pushcart Prize and the Rhysling Award. Her work has appeared in *Apex, Mythic Delirium,* and *Strange Horizons*, to name a few. She continues to write in between managing her business and taking care of her three-year-old.

Cary Barney   *Applause / After*

Cary was born in New York, raised in Massachusetts, and has lived in Spain since 1991. He teaches writing and theater at Saint Louis University's Madrid campus. His poems have appeared in *Tipton Poetry Journal, Third Wednesday, Quail Bell Review, Danse Macabre,* and *Big Windows*. His new collection *"Maritxu: A Love Story"* is forthcoming from Lemon Street Press.

Michael Belmore   *In These Times We Keep*

story of my life? .... too short for Kindle ... too long for a bumper sticker

Parul Bhargava   *the walk*

Parul is a physician who works at UCSF.

Henry Bladon   *The world changed*

Henry is a writer based in Somerset in the UK. His work can be seen in *The Poetic Bond* and other places.

Micki Blenkush   *What if my surreal is your surreal?*

Micki lives in St. Cloud, MN and works as a social worker. mickiblenkush.com

Bartholomew Bolander   *Ophiostoma ulmi*

Bartholomew Wilson Bolander grew up in New England, where he studied English and American literature. He obtained his master's degree in Modern Philology from l'Università degli studi di Roma 'La Sapienza' in the Fall of 2019. He lives in Rome.

Amelia Bostic   *Exposed*

Amelia, a resident of North Carolina, has never met a dog she didn't like.

Roisin Boyle   *Not airborne / Leave Me Breathless*

Roisin is from Halifax, Nova Scotia. She has an MA in English and will be studying law in the fall.

Brandon SC Brewer   *Those Eyes of Mine*

Brandon is a writer from Belleville, Illinois.

Cindy Lynn Brown   *Shutdown*

Cindy is a Danish-American poet. She has published nine books and has been translated into multiple languages, She is also the organizer of an international poetry festival.

Peter Bruno   *Cyanthropic Daze*

Peter Bruno is an artist, teacher, and writer living in Vermont. He also directs plays with high school students. Currently he is working on *"Garibaldi Avenue"*, a series of linked stories. He has two dogs, Bennie and Augie.

                         Field Notes from More Than Likely
Catherine Bull   *COVID19*

Catherine Bull is a poet living in Seattle, Washington. Her work has been published in FIELD, Bellingham Review, Literary Bohemian, and other journals. She has a full-length collection, *"Muskoxen Slow It Down"*, and chapbook, Rambo/Rimbaud.

Diane Burrow   *Routine*

Diane has been writing for many years and many of her poems are published in anthologies and booklets, including *The Poetic Bond* series. She is a regular contributor to *Poetry, Review and Discuss* on LinkedIN. She now lives by the sea.

Geraldine Moorkens Byrne   *When Will He Grow Wings / In Today's News*

Geraldine Moorkens Byrne is an author and poet from Dublin, Ireland. Her work has been published in a variety of anthologies, magazines, ezines and her work has been performed theatrically. Her first collection of poems *Dreams of Reality* was published in 2019.

Paola Caronni   *No Time for Spoon River*

Paola hails from Italy, lives in Hong Kong, where she works as a translator and tutor. MFA in Creative Writing (Hong Kong) ; MA in English Language and Literature (Milan). Her work has appeared in *Desde Hong Kong: Poets in Conversation with Octavio Paz, Quixotica: Poems East of La Mancha, Mingled Voices, Voice and Verse, Cha, 'New Asian Writing'* and on the 'PEN Hong Kong' website.

Mari-Carmen Marin   *This is War / Life in the Time of Coronavirus*

Born in Málaga, Spain, but moved to Houston, TX, in 2003, where she has found her second home. She is a professor of English at Lone Star College—Tomball. Writing poetry is her version of a comfy chair in front of a fireplace on a stormy winter day. Her work has appeared in *Wordriver Literary Review, Scarlet Leaf Review, Dash Literary Journal, Months to Years, The Awakening Review* and *Lucky Jefferson* .

Susana H Case *Sheltering*

Susana is a Professor at New York Institute of Technology, and author of seven books of poetry including *Dead Shark on the N Train* due out 2020 from Broadstone Books, Ippy Award winning *Drugstore Blue* (Five Oaks Press) as well as five chapbooks, among these are *Body Falling* and *Sunday Morning*, (Milk and Cake Press). Her first collection, *The Scottish Café*, from Slapering Hol Press, was re-released in a dual-language English-Polish version (Opole University Press). Also published in *Calyx, The Cortland Review, Portland Review, Potomac Review, Rattle, RHINO* and many other journals.

Benjamin Champagne *Cosmic Awareness*
Benjamin Champagne lives in a strange and changing world. It is ruled by patterns unseen and a very few who turn the cogs. Life is charming: coconut is a fine phonetic concoction. Life is chaotic: bamboozle sounds like what it means.

Conrad Spenser Clark *Not a Number*
Conrad a math postgrad dabbling in poetry, looking for crossovers in form. He also likes to paint abstract art, and has a small dog named, Pablo. This is his first published poem.

David Cleveland *Looking for Normal*
David Cleveland is an English Instructor at Arizona State University.

Kurt Cole Eldsvig *In and Out of Quarantine with Persephone*
Kurt is an artist and poet. His work has appeared in *Hanging Loose, Slipstream, Main Street Rag* and others. He maintains a website at www.EidsvigArt.com.

Hannah K Walizer Cook *Inside Out*
Hannah is a plant lover, writer, and poet who is passionate about creative expression, reading, personal growth, kindness and encouragement. She has been writing poems since the age of 15 to cope with loss, longing, love and depression.

Kristen Corbisiero   *Never-ending sun*

Kristen's poetry has been published by *Z Publishing House, Wildsound Festival Review, Poetry Festival, Serroc's Poetry Slam, Sage Express and Lighted Corners Literary Magazine*, among others. She discovered writing at an early age and clung to it as her means of expression through life. She earned a bachelor's degree in English and currently works as a social media coordinator and front-end manager. She enjoys photography, reading, and cultivating plants. She runs her own online blog, https://awriterssoulblog.wordpress.com/

Anna Delamerced   *Seeds in the Desert / Once More*

Anna is a medical student at the Warren Alpert Medical School of Brown University. She received funding through the Bray Medical Humanities Fellowship to pursue a year-long project, focusing on poetry for kids in the hospital. Her works have been published in K*evinMD, Medscape, Abaton, Plexus, in-Training, Cornerstone, Murmur* and *Doximity*. She is passionate about listening to people tell their stories.

Natasha N. Deonarain   *Social Distancing (speak to me)*

Natasha Deonarain's first chapbook, *50 etudes for piano*, will be published by Assure Press. She has been selected for the 2020 Three Sisters Award by NELLE magazine. Her work has appeared in T*he Inflectionist Review, Rogue Agent Journal, The Ravens Perch* and *Door is Ajar* among others. She lives between Colorado and Arizona, depending on weather patterns and sometimes practices medicine.

Abby DeSantis   *the morrow / the new normal*

Abby is a retired fashion executive from NYC, now residing in Northeastern Pennsylvania. She has found poetry to be her new passion. Abby has been published in *Northeastern PA Poetry Review 2020 Anthology, the 13 Days of Halloween,* and *Tiny Seeds Literary Journal.* She is a member of Poets Live Scranton and NEPA Pencils Writers.

Mitzi Dorton   *Shouldn't We Have Enough*

Mitzi has studied with both the Peripatetic Writing Workshops and Grubstreet. Mitzi's work has been published in *Rise, an Anthology of Change! Northern Colorado Writers,* and *Cleaning up Glitter,* as well as *'Bloodroot,'* and *'Good Old Days'* magazine. Mitzi worked as a learning specialist for the disabilities' center at a community college in the southeast. She loves scary dolls, with glass eyes from the turn of the century, local histories, and adventures with Marigold, her golden 'doodle.

Mike Dunne   *Shop-fever*

Michael Dunne grew up in Manchester but has lived in London for most of his adult life. He has had poetry published in *Wasafiri, Transmission, Lamport Court, Turbulence, Goldfish*, is included on the Poetry Society's website and in the Poetry Map of Manchester. Non-fiction has appeared in *London Irish Writer, NME, The Irish Post* and he is a past winner of the Chapter One Novel Writing Competition. He successfully completed an MA in Creative Writing at Goldsmiths, London, and is currently preparing a PhD proposal. He is a secondary school English teacher and works in alternative education with young people excluded from school.

Aaluk Edwardson   *Lockdown*

Aaluk Edwardson is an Iñuit/Norwegian/Sámi artist (writer, actor, director, singer). She also teaches creative writing and performance with Iḷisaġvik College, Alaska's only tribal college and serves as the Artistic and Executive Director of Bright Shores Creative Decolonization (BSCD). You can learn more about Aaluk and the work she does on the BSCD website: http://www.creativedecolonization.org.

| Jane Ellen Glasser | *Covid-19 Lockdown / Vernal Equinox Lockdown* |

Jane's poetry has appeared in journals, such as *Hudson Review, Southern Review, Virginia Quarterly Review* and *Georgia Review.* She co-founded the non=profit arts organization and journal New Virginia Review, and has worked as a book reviewer and editor. Her first collection *Naming the Darkness*, (introduction by W. D. Snodgrass) was issued by Road Publishers in 1991. She won the Tampa Review Prize for Poetry 2005 for *Light Persists* and *The Long Life* won the Poetica Chapbook Contest in 2011. Publications include *The Red Coat (2013), Cracks (2015), In the Shadow of Paradise (2017)* and *"Selected Poems" (2019)* all available from Future Cycle Press. Website: www.janeellenglasser.com

| **Brian M Falconer** | *'tween times* |

Brian M Falconer is an ex-computer programmer, now freelance technical and content writer, who recently won First Prize for his poem "Survival" in the anthology *Nature 20/20*. He also won third prize in the Poets' Choice Awards for *The Poetic Bond IX*, which may sound like a community chest card in Monopoly, but it was the first time he had won anything. He describes his style as "broken verse", and recently moved to Wales to be by the sea.

| **Catherine (Lee) Felty** | *Speak to me of new* |

Lee Felty is a published nature poet living in New England, USA.

| **Kristin Kowalski Ferragut** | *When screens replace touch* |

Kristin lives in Maryland where she has been a featured poet at readings including Words Out Loud at Glen Echo, Evil Grin in Annapolis, DiVerse Gaithersburg Poetry and Third Thursday Poetry Reading in Takoma Park. Kristin participates in local poetry and prose writing workshops and open mics, in addition to reading, hiking, teaching, playing guitar and enjoying time with her children. Her work has appeared in *Beltway Quarterly, Nightingale and Sparrow, Bourgeon* and *Mojave He[Art] Review* among others.

Hugh Findlay   *Go*

Hugh Findlay lives in Durham, NC, and would rather be caught fishing. He drives a little red MG, throws darts on Thursdays, reads and writes a lot, dabbles in photography and makes a pretty good gumbo. His work has been published in T*he Dominion Review, Literary Accents, Tiny Seed Literary Journal, Bangalore Review, Burningword Literary Journal, Wanderlust, Montana Mouthful, Souvenirs, Dream Noir, San Pedro River Review, Proem, New Southern Fugitives, Arachne Press* and *Pinesong.* @hughmanfindlay

Jen Finstrom   *Isolation Poem with Ceres*
                                  Isolation Poem with The Destruction of Pompeii

Jennifer was the poetry editor of *Eclectica Magazine* for thirteen years, and recent publications include *Gingerbread House Literary Magazine, Red Eft Review,* and *Thimble,* with work forthcoming in *Dime Show Review, Eunoia Review,* and *Rust + Moth.* Her work also appears in several Silver Birch Press anthologies, including *Ides: A Collection of Poetry Chapbooks.*

Carol Flake Chapman   *Maybe we will all become butterflies*
                                  A Prayer for the Sequestered

A former journalist, Carol returned to poetry, her first love, after the sudden death of her husband, on a wild river in Guatemala, shattered her world. Poetry, she found, was the language she needed to respond to a world gone haywire and badly in need of healing. She lives in Austin, Texas.

Andreas Fleps   *When The Music Begins*
Andreas Fleps is a 28-year-old poet, based near Chicago. He studied Theology and Philosophy at Dominican University, and has appeared or is forthcoming in publications such as *High Shelf Press, Snapdragon, The Windhover,* and *Waxing & Waning*, among others. Battling Major Depressive Disorder and Generalized Anxiety Disorder since the age of five, he translates teardrops.

Susan Fleming   *All Back in Place*

Susan Fleming is a real estate investor who grew up in the Appalachian area of Ohio. She has always been a big fan of poetry and enjoys writing personal poems in her spare time.

Pam Fox   *Black Swan Song*

Pam Fox is a professor of Religious Studies, Literature, and Humanities and co-founder of Perelandra College (www.perelandra.edu), formerly granting licensed, accredited Master's degrees in Creative Writing and now a certificate program, and has published numerous essays and poetry in academic journals.

Tanya Fraser   *Wide Berth*

Tanya lives in Brooklyn with her cat, Juno.

Mysti Frost   *#lifeinthetimeofcoronavirus*

Lives in Eugene, Oregon with her daughter Alice and father, the famous John Frost, a master storyteller.

Emma Gibson   *the dishes*

Emma is a British writer, now living in Philadelphia, PA. She mostly writes plays. Her most recent play, *WHEN WE FALL*, is a finalist for PlayPenn 2020, a semi-finalist for The Eugene O'Neill Conference, and a semi-finalist for Premiere Stages at Keane. She is also a teacher, a mother. and an actor.

Julia Gordon-Bramer *Rights / Seduction by Virus*

Julia Gordon-Bramer is a poet, author, Sylvia Plath scholar and professional tarot card reader. She quarantines in St. Louis, MO, with her husband and three cats.

Wendy Grossman *3/11/20*

Wendy is a creative non-fiction writer and author of the blog on race, www.wendyjanesoulshake.com. She also writes poetry using her friends' Facebook status updates. Publications: *Frequency Anthology, Missing Providence (2015,), Me and Mrs. Stowe* and *The Rhode Island Writers' Circle Anthology (2007). This poem was includes found Facebook status updates from the following with from* Barbara Gavin. Lily J. Whelan, Christopher Johnson, Martinha Javid, Darlene Sochin-Maras. ShaRhonda Knott-Dawson. Seth Tourjee. Shey Rivera. Rodney Mason and Jessica Brown

Blakelee Harmon *Podcast*

Blakelee Harmon is an established artist based in New York City who has dedicated her life to creating work that bonds human souls. She developed her sense of composition first through dance, exploring movement and stillness, music and silence, light and darkness, giving and taking, boundaries and abandon. .

Rob Hardy *Crossing the Delaware*

Rob Hardy is the first Poet Laureate of Northfield, Minnesota (USA). His prose and poetry have appeared in *New England Review, North Dakota Quarterly, New Letters, Ploughshares, The Critical Flame, Sonora Review, Pleiades, Rattle* and in other literary and scholarly journals and anthologies.

Michael Hatchett *unwitting conquests*
Hardly an Apocalypse in Here

Michael Hatchett is a writer in Chicago, Illinois. He graduated from the College of Wooster with a BA in English and the Second City Conservatory. He has work forthcoming from Thurston Howl Publications.

Syble Heffernan *Day 16 of Quarantine: Breathe*
Day 18 of Quarantine: Perspectves

Syble studies International Studies and English at Nebraska Wesleyan University. She started writing to entertain herself in small town Nebraska and filled countless journals on buses and garden benches during her year as an exchange student in Brazil. She participates in Spoken Word and is employed by the Nebraska Writers Collective. In addition to writing, she loves to read, dance, swim (especially in the sea), dig her toes in the dirt, paint and eat stovetop popcorn with coconut oil and pink Himalayan salt.

Camille Hill *After The Pandemic*

Ms. Hill is a retired U.S. diplomat. She grew up in Sacramento, CA, and lives in Van Zandt, WA.

Isabel Hinchliff *In sickness and in health*

Isabel Hinchliff is an English Major and intended Creative Writing Minor studying at UC Berkeley.

Nicole Hospital-Medina   *Backpacks*

Nicole earned her MFA at the University of Miami where she is now a professor who instructs writing. Her poems can be read in the anthologies *Feminine Rising: Voices of Power and Invisibility and Women Write Resistance: Poets Resist Gender Violence,* as well as in *CURA: A Journal of Art and Action, The Miami Herald, Linden Lane Magazine, Paper Nautilus, Blunderbuss Magazine, The Acentos Review, Canyon Voices* and more. Nicole, professor, Floridian, surfer, sailor, artist and environmentalist, ventures to write. She is a poet-activist.

Eric Machan Howd   *Stuck in the Funhouse*

Eric Machan Howd (Ithaca, NY) is a professor of professional and technical writing at Ithaca College. His poems have appeared in (selected) *Nimrod, River City, The Healing Muse,* and *Yankee Magazine.* He received his MFA in Creative Writing (Poetry) from the Vermont College of Fine Arts. He recently presented his work at a Slovenian/American conference on poetry and poetics as a guest lecturer/poet in Ljubljana, Slovenia.

Heikki Huotari   *In My Solitude*

Heikki, a retired math professor, has published poems in journals such as Spillway, The Journal, and Pleiades.

Kim June Johnson   *During My Illness / Blossoms*

Kim is an award-winning singer-songwriter and poet from the west coast of Canada. She is a recent graduate of Simon Fraser University's The Writer's Studio. Her writing has appeared in *Room, Literary Mama, CV2, and Today's Parent Magazine.*

Tonia Kalouria   *Looking Up*

Tonia wants to help reinstate RHYMING poetry from its Rodney Dangerfield "no respect" status. She is the author of the rhythmic *Aerobic Poetry*. Her poem *Advice is for the Birds* appears in the Poe Anthology, *Quoth the Raven*.

Judit Katalin Hollos   *Spring postponed - a Haiku Sequence*

Judit is a teacher, poet, playwright, translator and journalist. She graduated in playwriting and screenplay writing and studied Swedish literature and language in Vaxjö, Sweden. Her short stories, micro-poems, translations and articles have been featured in English, Swedish and Hungarian in literary magazines and anthologies.

H anonymous   *breathe*

Last minute replacement due to circumstances beyond control of the editors.

Alyssa Kreikemeier   *Eleven Days*

Alyssa Kreikemeier is a writer and historian whose work explores the relations between non-human and human worlds.

                                      Dog Walking in the Global Pandemic
Dorie LaRue   *Grocery Shopping Whole Foods*

Dorie LaRue is the author of two novels, *Resurrecting Virgil*, (Backwaters), and *The Trouble With Student Affairs (*Artemis Press); three chapbooks of poetry, *Seeking the Monsters, The Private Frenzy, In God's Due Time: A Tribute to Mistress Rowlandson*; poetry books *Mad Rains* (Kelsay Press), and *An Enemy in Their Mouths* (Finishing Line Press). Ahas appeaered in a variety of journals including, *The Southern Review, The Maryland Poetry Review,* and *The American Poetry Review.* Has a Ph.D. in creative writing from the University of Louisiana at Lafayette. She lives in Shreveport, Louisiana, and teaches writing and literature at LSUS.

Shane Leavy *Reflecting on another time of separation*

Shane Leavy is an analyst and writer living in the rural west of Ireland.

Christa Lubatkin *What if*

Christa Lubatkin was born in war, raised through post-war poverty and finally landed in the country of everyone's dreams, where she moved and moved again. For someone who never lingers long, writing short poetry is a natural fit. Christa's poetry shines a light on darkness. Her poetry has appeared in T*he Patterson Literary Review, Haunted Waters Press (Splash), The Blue Guitar, The Write Launch, Underwood, Cathexis Northwest,* and others. Away from her writing table she likes to hike, dance, and enjoy the company of good people.

Neetu Malik *Social Distancing (every two minutes)*

Born in India, Neetu has lived in Austria, England, and Canada before settling in the Eastern USA in 1994. Neetu's eclectic work reflects her diverse background as she explores the joy and darkness of the human condition in poems and stories noteworthy for their intensity in brief span. Her poetry is published in journals and anthologies from Australia, USA, UK, and India, inlcuding *The Poetic Bond* and others. Her poem, *Soaring Flames*, was awarded First-Place by the NY Literary Magazine (2017). Nominated for the Pushcart Prize in 2018, Neetu's poem *Sacred Figs* was published in The Ocotillo Review by Kallisto Gaia Press.

Susan Manchin *Now That You're Gone*

A graduate of West Virginia University, worked as a copywriter and creative director. Presently, pursuing an MFA in creative writing at Bennington College with a focus on poetry. She is an active member of Pennwriters and SCBWI. Most recently, she completed workshops at Highlights, and Stony Brook University.

Kayla Matheson *Prison Life*

A retired English teacher from Texas, Kayla has shared her love of poetry with her students for nineteen years. She has been published in *The Poetic Bond IV, the Poetic Bond IX*, and two articles and poems in *Poet's Are Heroes* Magazine.

Johnnie Clemens May   *Inundated*

Johnnie Clemens May, a Phoenix area poet, has an MFA from Pacific University and taught poetry and creative writing at the college level for over 25 years. She has also conducted many workshops and participated in several readings in her community as well as having published her work in a number of journals and online literary magazines.

Annmarie McQueen   *We didn't think it would be us next*

English, Creative Writing graduate from Warwick University in the U.K, Previously a winner of the Simon Powell poetry prize and has been published in magazines including *'Words with Jam,' 'Reach poetry'* and *'Buried letter press.'*

Mary K O'Melveny   *Space Bubbles / Adrenaline Rush*

Mary K O'Melveny (Washington DC and Woodstock NY): is author of *A Woman of a Certain Age* and *MERGING STAR HYPOTHESES*.

Anthony Mirarcki   *Moments of Life / 100,000*

Anthony Mirarcki lives in Syracuse, New York, with his wife. He currently works as a carpenter and is a full-time student at Oswego State University, working towards his BA in English with a minor in Philosophy. Anthony's work has appeared in the *Great Lake Review*, and earned honorable mention in the 47th New Millennium Writing Awards

KAT Milberger   **What is left**

Kat has been a social worker working with the autism spectrum population for 9 years in Richmond, Virginia. She is proud member of the LGBTQ community and the fluidity of my experience has informed my poetry; poetry sets free the conventions of speech and writing. On March 16th, 2020, she developed a fever, had to leave work, and proceeded to experience the rest of her illness in self-quarantine. She says "Covid-19 is unlike anything I have experienced; the way that it improves and then suddenly worsens, see-sawing back and forth for days and days, is maddening. It steals the air from our lungs and causes us to labor over each breath; in and out. Experiencing this in isolation, before good information was available to the public about it, hit on many of my core fears as a human being; I am corrupt, I am a burden, I am bound to be rejected, I am useless. It was these voices, and the eventual recovery of my health and self-love, that inspired my poetry."

Justin Moir

The Song is Quiet Now / To A Plague Rat

Justin Moir is a writer and English graduate student from Halifax.

Kristina Moriconi   *#quarantineartclub*

Kristina Moriconi is a poet and essayist whose work has appeared in a variety of literary journals and magazines including B*revity, Cobalt Review, Ruminate*, as well as many others. Her work has also been selected as a finalist in terrain.org's 2017 Nonfiction Contest, December's 2018 & 2019 Curt Johnson Prose Award in Nonfiction, and awarded Honorable Mention in Juncture's 2018 Memoir Contest. Future publications include *Sonora Review: the Woodhall Press anthology,* and *Flash Nonfiction Food (2020)*.Her lyrical narrative, In the *Cloakroom of Proper Musings*, will be published by Atmosphere Press in 2020.

Kohl Neal   *The end of the world from inside the house*

Kohl Neal is a writer and advocate born in New Jersey, raised in Texas, living and in Chicago.

Maxine Nodel   *United States of Virus*

Has a BFA in Fine Art from Cooper Union and an MFA in Creative Writing from Brooklyn College. She studied writing privately with Allen Ginsberg in the late 80s and received an award from the Academy of American Poets for original poetry. Founded my own art high school in NYC with a Bill and Melinda Gates Foundation grant in 2003. The school received the 2009 Lincoln Center Institute 1st Place Award for the Most Imaginative Curriculum in NYC. She has also written educational material, including for the Children's Television Workshop.

Bridget Noel   *And's and But's of Quarantine / Just A Nurse*

Bridget Noel is an alumnus of Rutgers University and the University of Pennsylvania. She received the Mitchell Adelman Memorial Scholarship for Creative Writing at Rutgers University. She is currently a critical care nurse.

Vox Pop Max Pax   *Prepped*

(Nathan Carmen Brown) British/American Citizen, New York native, traveled in Europe and Australia, and until now, across the United States of America. Hold up in the midwest until the virus passes.

JOHN PIETARO   *A Fallout Unspoken*
Writer, poet, spoken word artist and musician from Brooklyn NY, and staff columnist/critic of the *NYC Jazz Record,* Recently commissioned for *Shifting the Jazz Narrative: Photo Essays of Women Instrumentalists* by the Berklee Institute for Jazz and Gender Justice. Curates the poetry/music series West Village Word at Cafe Bohemia NYC. Other recent credits include poetry in *Il Biglietto 2*" (translated by Erika Dagnino, Genoa Italy: Sibello, 2018), the proletarian fiction collection *Night People and Other Tales of Working New York*" (2013). Contributing writer to *Z, the Nation, CounterPunch, the Wire (UK), People's World* and other progressive and arts periodicals.

Peter Prizel   *N-95*

Anthony Chesterfield (aka. Peter Prizel) is a social worker who specializes in end-of-life care and hospice. Each of his patients and their families have individually taught him about the unknown as he continues his vocation. Anthony considers fatherhood to be the greatest adventure of his life, and believes there is no one perfect way to be a father. He is currently pursuing an MFA at Manhattanville College, and lives in Bedford Hills, NY, with his wife, three daughters, and three cats.

MK Punky   *Pandemic Possibilities*

MK PUNKY is the author of many books, including the novel *Year 14* (Barrelhouse Books), and gambling memoir "*The Smart Money* (Simon & Schuster), as well as his beloved travelogue-with-dog *Ella in Europe* (Bantam/Dell). MK's memoir of befriending and housing a homeless man, *The Unexpected Guest* (Diversion), is forthcoming in 2020.

Monica Raymond   *Corona Pantoum*
Monica Raymond writes poems, plays, and sometimes prose. She's currently sheltering in place in an old house in Cambridge, Massachusetts. She wrote this poem in February, before the quarantine.

Barbara Reynolds *Once Upon a Children's' Game / A Pandemic Day*

Barbara Reynolds' poems have appeared in W*hat Rough Beast, Avocet, Muddy River Poetry Review,* and *The Somerville Times.*

Laurie Rosen *Tiny Bay*

Laurie Rosen lives near the coast in Massachusetts. She is inspired by travel, nature, politics and the myriad photographs she takes of her surroundings. This poem was written while she was out of the country though practicing self-quarantine. She left for home just before all flights were cancelled. Her poems have appeared in *Sisyphus, Tigershark Magazine, The London Reader, Rosette Maleficarum, The Muddy River Review, Beach Reads,* and *Peregrine.*

Robert Eugene Rubino *Pretend You're a Dangerous Dissident Make an Effort, Make Your Bed*

Since retiring from daily journalism in 2013, Robert Eugene Rubino has published poetry and prose in various online and print literary journals, including *Hippocampus, The Esthetic Apostle, The Write Launch, Haunted Waters Press, Forbidden Peak Press, Cagibi, Cathexis Northwest, High Shelf Press, Raw Art Review, MacQueen's Quinterly,* and *Gravitas*, as well as anthologies *The Poetic Bond IX* and *Earth Hymn*. Since the shelter-in-place order in response to the coronavirus, he has shifted his participation in poetry open mics from in-person to online, believing something is better than nothing.

Nida Sahar *Isolation / Lockdown Pheromone*

Started writing poetry at the age of 13, influenced by Sufi poets like Rumi. She has a Bachelor of Engineering degree in Information Technology from BMSCE, Bangalore, but after years of being a closet poet, she eventually sjoined a poetry workshop at Bangalore Writers She has written for online portals such as Women's Web, and Career sites like Shiksha, and newspapers like Deccan Herald. Her poetry is published in *MuseIndia, Coldnoon (International Journal of Travel Writing & Travelling Cultures), Spark.* and *FWDLife.* She performs at a few open mics and explores different poetic forms. She has also won a competition from *Let poetry be and* is a featured poet for Bengaluru Poetry Festival. She is a feminist and a firm supporter of women in engineering and technology.

Laura Saint Martin

The Hunkering Down
....

Laura is an emerging writer, working on a mystery series set in the foothills of Southern California, featuring horses and their eccentric but brave owners. She also writes poetry about life on the autism spectrum, mental health, blue collar struggles, and animals and nature.

Heather Sanderson *grasp-less*

Heather Sanderson is a healer and yoga teacher focusing on reclaiming the sacred feminine and invisible wounds. Originally from Canada by way of Brooklyn, she has lived nomadically since 2017 and has moved 160 times. Her work has appeared in *NightBlock.* Writing is her medicine.

Nancy Santos *When Anagrams Great Again*

Nancy Santos is complying with stay-at-home orders in Washington with her husband and two sons.

Susan Sanders *Five Directions for Surviving Covid-19*

In addition to publishing a book and several poems over the past 30 years, Susan has taught English and Humanities classes for two Vermont colleges, as well as juggling two to three part-time jobs since returning to Vermont after 9/11. She lives on the edge of a lake which borders Vermont and Quebec. Poetry is the one avenue which greatly allowed some reprieve after her daughter's suicide several years ago. Her poems have appeared in *The Vermont Literary Review, Flying Horse, Thin Air, Falling Star Magazine, The Lucid Stone, Green Mountains Review, Soapbox, Ariel Chart, Scarlet Leaf Review* and several others.

Sophie Scolnik-Brower *Click*

Sophie Scolnik-Brower is a professional pianist and social work student in the Boston area. An active participant in writing workshops throughout the city, she is drawn to poetry that sounds like music. Past and current writing mentors include Jorie Graham, Katia Kapovich, and Tom Daley.

Barbara Schwegman   *Pandemic*

Barbara has been a writer of poetry her entire life, but have never felt comfortable sharing with anyone other than her close friends. Last night she was practicing social distancing by porch sitting with friends, and shared *Pandemic* with them. They encouraged me to share it with a larger audience. So here we are, Thank you.

Helen Sheppard   *Bubbles in a War Zone*

Helen writes poems about birth and for those unheard.She co-runs Satellite of Love Word Events and enjoys the alchemy of giving new poets a platform to showcase their words. Published in*: These are the Hands 2020, Lyrically Justified Volume 3, 2019 Tools of the Trade – Poems for New Doctors* (2019), Readings/performances include *Milk Poetry, Raise the Bar, Torriano Meeting house, Harvard Medical School.* Helen was commended in the *Hippocrates Prize* 2017 https://www.writeoutloud.net/profiles/helensheppard

Richard Glen Smith   *Intubed*

As an artist and media specialist, worked for 40 years on disease and AIDS issues with media, medical, and health specialists. After retirement he found himself confronted with lung issues which extend directly into the present pandemic and its effect on societies.

Sara Cupp Smith   *Shelter in Place / Intubation*

Sara has retired from urban life. She lives with her husband, Italian Spinone, and five jennies on forty mostly wooded acres in a rural area of eastern Texas. There she enjoys the rich variety of wildlife, including foxes, cougars, raccoons, deer, beavers, owls, hawks, and songbirds and tolerates possums, feral hogs, copperheads, and an occasional alligator. Her other pleasures include watching the changing foliage of the oak and hickory trees, reading long books, and drinking coffee each morning. She treasures her husband, two children, daughter-in-law, son-in-law, and five grandchildren.

Samantha Smith   *Paranoid Hopeless Romantic*

Samantha resides in Berea, Kentucky. She attends Eastern Kentucky University and will graduate in Spring 2021.

Danielle Solo   *Social Distancing (eyes like prey) / Quarantine Routine*

Danielle Solo is a poet and storyteller based in London, Ontario. She defines artistic expression as a form of radical honesty. Her work focuses on spirituality and traumatic personal experience, uncovering the hauntings that result from these events. Her poetry can be found in works by *Polemical Zine and Jawbreaker Collective,* and is forthcoming in *Mineral Lit Mag.* It's not hard to spot her in the wild; she's the most eccentric person in your grocery store, often found swathed in velvet and discussing mortality with the tanked lobsters. She can be found on Instagram @daniellesoloscribblings or at daniellesolo.com.

Megha Sood   *Redemption / Looking Outside*

Megha Sood is an Assistant Poetry Editor at Ariel Chart and MookyChick. Over 350+ works in print/online journals. Works in 35 anthologies by the US, UK, Australian, and Canadian Press. Two-time State-level winner of the NJ Poetry Contest 2018/2019.

Samantha Stone   *An Echo Through Pelagic*

Samantha is an illustrator and emerging writer living among the redwoods of Northern California

Linda Stryker   *Actually*

Linda writes from Phoenix, AZ. She volunteered for many years as a radio reader for disabled people. She founded the poetry groups Poetry Exchange, for critiquing work, and COW: Community of Writers. She also participates in a ZOOM poetry critique/workshop with members from all across the U.S. Stryker has been published in *New Millennium Writings, New Verse News, Ekphrastic Review, Antiphon,* and *Chiron Review*, among several others. Her chapbook *Starcrossed* was published in 2018 and she is currently working on a new collection. She continues to try to crack the mystery of how to write a darned good poem.

Jacky T   *Battered Ego*

Jacky T is a country boy at heart, wearing city life like an itchy woollen sweater. He battles chronic illness, so currently feels at home with the world's preoccupations.

Claire Taylor   *The Lilac Bush / To My Son*

Claire Taylor is a writer and Licensed Massage Therapist. Her poetry has appeared in *The Yellow Arrow Journal,* and *The Loch Raven Review.*

Loretta Tobin   *Let's all dance in the street / Waiting Alone*

Born and raised in North Dakota, graduated from Minnesota State University Moorhead with a B.S.Ed. and now lives in Snohomish County, Washington. While married, she raised two children, and joined the U.S. Navy Reserve and served around the world including Al Asad, Iraq. When asked why she volunteered, she answers that she was gathering material to use for award winning writing. Now retired, she looks forward to bringing those influences into her writing.

Amy Walker   *A Cadence inverted*

Amy is a multi-genre writer and international development practitioner. She has published previously in *Northern New England Review* and *Midway Journal.* She wrote this piece in the weeks when Italy was suffering the worst of COVID-19 infections and deaths and the virus had begun to spread widely throughout the U.S. She was moved watching the images of Italians and Spaniards making music from their balconies and Yo-Yo Ma serenading the world from his home office, like independent and fragile notes composing a global nocturne. She is sheltering-in-place in Washington, D.C. with her husband and chocolate Labrador.

Wen Wen Lin   *Life in The Time of Covid-19*

Wen Wen Lin is a transplant to New York City who feeds off nature, enjoy crowd-less city streets in early mornings or very late at night. She catches the tail of inspiration solely with mobile phones.

Gemma Webster   *Essential*

Gemma Webster is a Colorado writer. She is a contributing editor at FictionUnbound.Com and is a graduate of the Lighthouse Writer's Workshop Book Project.

Nicole Williams   *The Thing with no Form*

Nicole Williams is a graduate of UT Austin. She's been a law student, an event planner, a florist, a home school teacher, a Bible study leader, an encourager, a vice president of operations, and a writer. She loves God's word and its incredible power to change our lives. With every word she writes, she hopes people will hear the underlying message: God is real, He is able, and He loves you.

Patricia Williams   *Thoughts at the time of the virus - Pandemic*

Patricia Williams' collection, *Midwest Medley*, published in 2018 by Kelsay Books was named Outstanding Poetry Book by the Wisconsin Library Association.

Nan Williamson   *Spring 2020 / Bouleversée*

Graduate of The Humber School for Writers (Toronto) 2013. Since then, my poems have been published in *Room, The Steel Chisel, Mindshadows, Arborealis,* as well as *Three Drops* (Cauldron), and th e2017 best of print anthology from Imbolc (UK). Her chapbook, *leave the door open for the moon*,was published by Jackson Creek Press, Peterborough, Ontario, 2015. Her poem *Georgian Bay Meditation* was one of 15 chosen by the League of Canadian Poets for the April 30th 2020 Poem in your Pocket Day.

Maili Woods   *Tsunami*

Mali Woods-Drake is a union representative for hospital employees in California. As a former English major/creative writing minor, writing has been a cathartic release during the stressful times.

Susana Molinolo and Pamela Yuen-Elkerbout   *Postcards We Never Sent*

Susana Molinolo is an Argentine born, Toronto-based copywriter and activist. In 2017 her poem, I Am Nine, was a winner in the Ontario Books Publishers' Association writing contest. She is currently the Programming Chair for the Toronto branch of Canadian Authors Association.

Pamela Yuen-Elkerbout was born in rural Ontario to Hong Kong migrants. She is an expressive writing facilitator with the Toronto Writers Collective. Her writing explores diasporas, normativity, kinship, and mysticism.

Susana and Pamela first met on Twitter, and then in real life at the Tartan Turban Secret Reading Series in Toronto. As their workplaces are close by, they had planned to meet for lunch until COVID-19 cancelled all socializing. In lieu of a face-to-face lunch, they wrote this poem together as an imagined meeting in New York City.

M Zaman   *Anthropocene Sin / Hope*

A poet and an physician; he lives with his lovely wife on the Raquette River in a quaint college town on the foothills of the majestic Adirondacks, enchantingly irenic with rivulets full of toothsome water, and hills rarely trodden. His poems are published or forthcoming in the *High Shelf Press, the Stardust Review, the Black Horse Review,* and the *Cathexis North West Press, Ulalame Lighthouse,* and *La Piccioletta Barca.* He also writes in his native language Bangla. His most recent publication in Bangla is a translation of the *Epic of Gilgamesh.*

Cigeng Zhang   *The Frozen Spring*

Cigeng is a freelance English translator from China. Her poetic contributions include her poems in *The Poetic Bond III to IX (2013 - 2019), as well as Rouge in the Water,* her first bilingual poetry collection published in China in 2017.

Felucia Zuniga   *Inside and Outside / Old words, New Tricks*

Felicia Zuniga is currently trapped in her home with her husband and her two-year-old son as she continues to work as a communications specialist and attempts to write poetry and keep the house clean. Learn more on her website at: www.feliciazuniga.com.

Trevor Maynard (editor, The Lockdown)

Trevor has three poems featured in this collection *troubadours of the scaffold; The World Has Changed, But There is Hope;* and *This Spring.*

He has several published collections including *The Path Now Known, Grey Sun Dark Moon,* and *Keep on Keepin' On,* as well as his one-act play anthology *Four Truths.*

He has been the editor of the international poetry anthology series *The Poetic Bond* since 2011 and will publish *The Poetic Bond X* in late 2020. So far, *The Poetic Bond* has showcased the work of 223 poets from 35 countries. This year he also edited *Nature 20/20*, an anthology of 21 poets on the theme of the environment.

Trevor is also the editor of the Cunningham Short Story Anthologies *Life Dances (2017)* and *Our World, Your Place (2018), Nine Frames (2019).*

Other publications featuring his work include **Aesthetica, Tuck, October Hill, Deep Underground, Poetry, Life and Times**, **Miracle,** and the anthology **Men in the Company of Women (EAP)**.

Trevor is a member of **The Poetry Society (UK)** and formerly an executive member of **The Writer's Guild of Great Britain**, and treasurer of **The Theatre Writers' Union.** He is the manager of the LinkedIn poetry forum **Poetry, Review, and Discuss**, which has 20,700 members.

265

The Poetic Bond
Series

What makes a
Poetic Bond?

The process of selecting poems for publication in
THE POETIC BOND series is unlike any other in that there is
no set plan as to what will be published. It depends on the
themes that emerge from the pool of work submitted, or to put
it another way, the poetic energy which comes together at this
certain time and place. Where themes emerge, patterns of
energy harmonize, bonds form, connections are made, these
in turn lead to interconnected chapters, and the creation of a
holistic volume, deeply connected with humanity, nature, and
the universe.

Reviews for The Poetic Bond Series

"Readers will feel joy, sorrow, and every emotion in between" Review of
PBVIII
"The poetry that fills this book is moving, deep, and affirming"
Nicholas Chiarkas (WI, USA)
"…very impressed with much of the excellently crafted writing "
Robin Hislop (UK/Spain)
" … a joy to read … thanks for creating this bond and including me in it"
Neetu Malik (PA, USA/India)

The Poets of the Poetic Bond I - IX *(2011-2019)*

George Chijioke Amadi, Victoria Anllo, Christine Anderes, Vesna Adriana Arsenich, Suzanne Askham, Pushpita Awasthi, Frances Ayers, **Maria Ivana Treviasani Bach,** *Chris Barras, Graham Bates, Elaine Battersby, Mark Beechill, Rebecca Behar, Gillian Bell, Annel Bell Martin, Janette Bendle,* **Nikki Bennett,** *Henry Bladon, Betty Bleen, J E Bird, Melissa Bird, Scott Pendragon Black, Joanne Bordokan, Beatrice Huerta Boswell, Lewis Bosworth, Marguerite Guzman Bouvard, Rosalind Brenner, Dan Brook, BJ Brown, Jessie Brown, Lexene Burns Krenare Burqi, Diane Burrow, Robert Campion, Mariangela Canzi, Bonnie Gail Carter, George Carter, Low Kwai Chee, Julie Clark, Alexander Clarke,* **Drew Claussen,** *Tim Coburn, Diane Colette, Ian Colville,* **Durand J. Compton,** *Clark Cook, Antonella Corradetti, Laurie Corzett, Flavia Cosma, Pedro Cuhna, James Darcy, Rick Davis, Rhona Davidson, Catherine DeWolf, William Di Benedetto, Sam Doctors, Marian Dunn, Belinda DuPret, Sumita Dutta, Amanda Eakins, Brian M Falconer, A.D.Fallon, Madelina Fine, Amber Jimenez-Flores, Gilbert A.Franke, Bonnie J. Flach, Nina Floreteng, Stuart Forrest, Louise Francois, Anthony Frobisher, Annette Gagliardi, Bea Garth, Annette Gagliardi, Edna George, James Gilmore, Ingrid Gjelsvik, Cathryn Glenday, Caroline Glenn, J.M. Greff, William Gregory, George K Grieve, Kelli Gunn, Peter Hagen, Sandra Hanks, Scott Hastie, Seamus Harrington, Karen Henneberry, James Higgins, Robin Ouzman Hislop, Chi Holder, Pamela Hope, Ann Huang, Rowland Hughes, Rachel Z Ikins, Romi Jain, Diane Jardel. Jane Johann, Michael Lee Johnson, Wendy Joseph, Amanda Valerie Judd, Sebastien Karatonis, Sajida Khan, Sonia Kilvington, Stephen Kirin, KishaJade, Justin Kribbe, Cathriona Laffert, John Lambremont Snr,*

Frieda W Landau, Lee Landau, Jill Angel Langlois, Shari-Jo LeKane-Yetumi, Laura Lee, Lawrence W. Lee, Mark L Levinson, Carey Link, Madeline Heit Lipton, Tatjana Loncarec, Marek Lugowski, Drake Mabry, Naomi Madelin, Neetu Malik, Christopher Maloney, Kayla Matheson, Chris Maynard, Luke Zachary Maynard (UK). Trevor Maynard, Brian McCully, Janice McLaughlin, John McMullen, Michael Melichov. Tania Melick, Miklos Mezosi, Claire Mikkelsen, Simon Miller, Linda Mills, Bilal Moin, Greg Mooney, Helen H. Moore, Marli Merker Moreira, Debbie Edwards Morton, Mustafa Munir, Sonay Mustafa, Hongvan, Nguyen Deborah Nyamekbe, Denisa Parsons, R.H. Peat, Jude Neale, Freddie Ostrovskis, Christine Pearson, Patricia Pfahl, Lizzie La Poole, Robert Prattico, Gillian Prew, Nancy Pritchard, Glen Proctor, Carrie Magness Radna, Sarah Rahman, Rainbow Reed, Bonnie Roberts, George C. Robertson, Reasie Robertson, Sayed H. Rohani, Karen Nurenberg Rotherstein, Biman Roy, Robert Eugene Rubino, Ivan Saltaric, Niek Satjin, Helen Schulman, Nancy Scott, Claude Sequy, Leander Seddon, Maja Herman Sekulic, Stephen Sesto, Gill C Shaw, Michael Shepherd, Sharla Lee Shults, Joseph J.Simmons, Joseph Sinclair, Richard Glen Smith, Pete Soron, Tom Spencer, Tom Sterner, Ashleigh Stevens, N. A'Yara, Stein Sarah Stonesifer, Fiona Sullivan, Paul Sutherland, James Sutton, Antony Taylor, Charles Thielman, Janet Gell Thompson, Nana Tokatli, Peter Coe Verbica, Kewayne Wadley, Diana Wend, Swaizi Vaughan, Wybrig J. De Vries, Brian Walker, Will Walsh, Tom Watts, Marcia Weber, Mark Jason Welch, Ann Widdicor, Tim Williams, Jim Wilson, Michaelle Yarborough, Terry Young, Marie Youssefirad, Cigeng Zhang, Lynne Zotalis

Poetry by Trevor Maynard

"Trevor B Maynard combines complicated thematic material and unites fractured images with a sure hand." (THE STAGE)

The Path Now Known

An intimate study of the frailties of life, the human condition. Symbolically, the passage of time is explored, from Sunrise to Morning, then Later, Dusk to Night.

Grey Sun. Dark Moon

An intimate study of the frailties of life, the human condition. Symbolically, the passage of time is explored, from Sunrise to Morning, then Later, Dusk to Night.

Keep on Keepin' On

A poetry work in five chapers: Black Dog, Panopticon, Observation, Loving, and Answers. Human is our condition, life is our journey, and come love, joy, agony, or world-weariness, let's just Keep on Keepin' On.

The Cunningham
Short Story Competition

To honour the life of his maternal grandfather, **Robert Hamilton Cunningham,** in 2017, Trevor Maynard set up a short story competition, the theme of which was for each story to open the reader's eyes to the wider world we live in.

2019 "Nine Frames"

Thumbs Up by Teri Bran, *The Race,*by Mike Friers (1st prize) *Misanthropes* by Dean Gessie, *White Flags* by R.D Girvan *Your Table is Ready* by Gregg Voss, *Elan* by Kevin M Patrick *Starlight* by Piet Pedersson, *Serious as a Heart Attack* by Lynne Zotalis, and featuring **George**, by Trevor Maynard
An honest diary of coping with age and continuing to live on.

2018 "Our World, Your Place"

Veiled by Rebecca Evans (1st prize) *The Seal* by Rebekah Dodson *The Bench* by Karen Quinnon, *Slim* by Tonya Walker *Of Strange Lands and People* by James Najarian *Sentenced to Life* by Oscar Heitmart *The Viet Kieu Casanova* by Tuan Phan *The World I Grew Up In* by Lynne Zotalis

2017 "Life Dances"

No Going Back by Sandy Norris (1st Prize)
Baking by Maria Borland, *When Food Kills* by Linda DuPret *The Death of Rock'n'Roll* by Michael McLaughlin *Too Much* by Israela Marglait, *True North* by Lynne Zotalis And featuring **The Dance** by Trevor Maynard.

Further Details available at www.willowdownbooks.com

The Poetic Bond Series
..." A beautiful publication that will rest on top of my favorite books of poetry." Nicholas Chiarkas (WI, USA)

"A wonderful collection of poetry that is made extra special in the fact that its writers come from all over the world"
MB (Amazon)

"A book to carry with you for moments of meditative thought"
Diane Jardel (Eire)

Life Dances
"Trevor Maynard's "The Dance" provides a fascinating, honest, and personal window into life during the war years and is equally matched by the short stories the competition set up around it inspired."
RM (Glasgow, UK)

Our World, Your Place
"I was very pleased by the quality of this book. I particularly liked the way that the stories are from writers all over the world which helps to bring people together. I would recommend this book to anyone who loves to read short stories."
Claire M (Amazon)

Nine Frames
"Romantic, magical, and authentic"
MD (Ontario, Canada)

"Every story is interesting, entertaining, and well-told. I will be buying more copies as Christmas presents for my family."
GG (California, USA)

Willowdown Books Catalogue

Poems from The Lockdown (2020)
146 poems from 115 poets across the world. As the pandemic rages, humanity is quarantined, but our poetic voices remain strong, and we will survive the Lockdown.
ISBN-13: 9798630190185

The Path Now Known (2020)
by Trevor Maynard
A collection of poems
ISBN: 9798606601561

Nature 20/20 (2020)
International poetry anthology, featuring Brian M Falconer, Konnie Risinger, Mariangela Canzi, and eighteen other poets. Edited by Trevor Maynard
ISBN-13: 9781658033138

Nine Frames (2019)
Piet Pedderson, Gregg Voss, Kevin Michael Patrick, Dean Gessie, R.D. Girvan, Mike Friers, Lynne Zotalis, Teri Bran, Trevor Maynard. Anthology of 9 short stories.
ISBN-13: 9781073411511

The Poetic Bond VIII (2018)
International poetry anthology
ISBN-13: 9781729531778

Our World, Your Place (2018)
Rebecca Evans, Tuan Phan, James Najarian, Rebekah Dodson, Lynne Zotalis, Oscar Heitmart, and Tonya Walker. An anthology of eight short stories, edited by Trevor Maynard
ISBN: 978-1727650686

The Poetic Bond VII (2017)
International poetry anthology
ISBN: 978-1978098039

Life Dances (2017)
Sandy Norris, Lynne Zotalis, Maria Borland, Michael
McLaughlin, Belinda DuPret, and Israela Margalit. An
anthology of six short stories edited by Trevor Maynard
ISBN: 978-1978098039

The Poetic Bond VI (2016)
International poetry anthology
ISBN: 978-1539334682

Echoes in the Earth (2016)
by Pushpita Awasthi
Collected poems edited by Trevor Maynard
ISBN: 978-1533618801

Grey Sun, Dark Moon (2015)
by Trevor Maynard
A collection of poems
ISBN: 978-1517095253

The Poetic Bond V (2015)
International poetry anthology
ISBN: 978-1517783808

The Poetic Bond IV (2014)
International poetry anthology
ISBN: 978-1503034525

The Poetic Bond III (2013)
International poetry anthology
ISBN: 978-1492384199

Keep on Keepin' On (2012)
by Trevor Maynard
A collection of poetry
ISBN: 978-1480052499

The Poetic Bond II (2012)
International poetry anthology
ISBN: 978-1480209732

The Poetic Bond (2011)
International poetry anthology
ISBN: 978-1466498419

Four Truths (2011)
by Trevor Maynard
Four one act plays (1989-1996)
"She", "From Pillow to Post", "Graye", and "Taciturn"
ISBN, 978-1466453395

From Pillow to Post (2010)
by Trevor Maynard
One-act play (1991)
ISBN 978-0955851414

Glass (2010)
by Trevor Maynard
A full length play (1996)
ISBN 978-1445233239

The Watcher from the Beacon (2010)
by Peter Alan Soron
Poetry collection by Trevor Maynard
ISBN-13: 978-1480108806

Love, Death, and the War of Terror (2009)
Poetry by Trevor Maynard
ISBN 978-1445206622

Love, light, and peace

276

Printed in Great Britain
by Amazon